DISPLACEMENT

BY LUCY KNISLEY

Executive Editor: Gary Groth
Senior Editor: J. Michael Catron
Copyeditor: Janice Lee
Production: Paul Baresh, Keeli McCarthy
Cover lettering: Keeli McCarthy
Associate Publisher: Eric Reynolds
Publisher: Gary Groth

Fantagraphics Books, Inc.
7563 Lake City Way NE • Seattle, WA 98115

First Fantagraphics Books edition: March 2015
ISBN 978-1-60699-810-6
Printed in China

To receive a free catalog of more books like this, as well as an amazing variety
of cutting-edge graphic novels, classic comic book and newspaper strip collections,
eclectic prose novels, uniquely insightful cultural criticism, and other fine works of
artistry, call (800) 657-1100 or visit fantagraphics.com.

Twitter: @fantagraphics • Facebook: facebook.com/fantagraphics

DISPLACEMENT

n. A measurment of a ship taken by the weight of water equal to a ship's underwater volume. The weight of a mass of water pushed aside by the intrusion of a ship's hull.

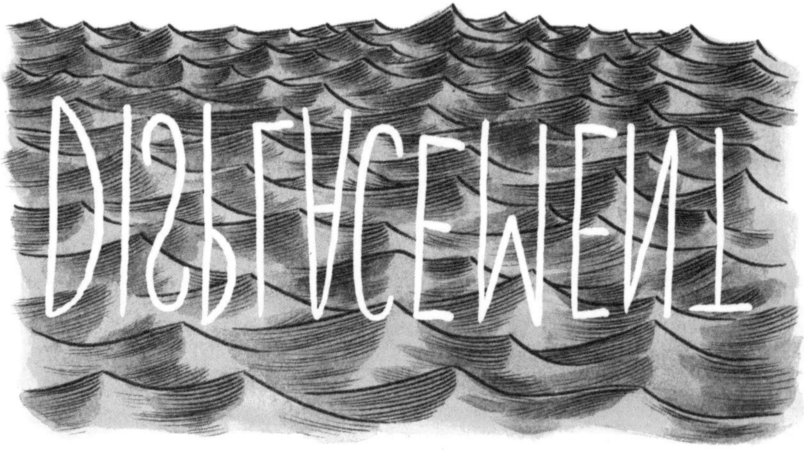
DISPLACEMENT

Introduction

In the period after I finished my last book, but before it was released, I decided to spend my time having adventures. I was still reeling from a breakup, but enjoying the rest from writing and drawing my newest graphic novel. I was lucky to ferret out offers to travel; a comic convention in Europe, a job as a counselor for study-abroad trips, paid travel writing...
And a cruise for the elderly.

In February of 2012, I accompanied my grandparents on board a cruise ship. I love my grandparents, but as many with loved ones in their 90s will tell you, travel and care-taking are no easy endeavor. This book is the journal of my experience.

I brought along my well-loved copy of my grandfather's war memoir. I thought it would be a conversation-starter, and a way to feel better connected to my somewhat taciturn grandparents. It turned out to be a close companion to me in the loneliness I felt at hiding my own terror and heartbreak at my grandparent's decline in health — in the book my grandparents, at my age, experience war and horror and love and adventure. It connected me to their history. Here is an excerpt from the introduction of his memoir, "Three Years Out of My Life."

"Recently a few memories of my time in the war have been triggered, and for my own gratification, I've decided to put some of the things I remember down on paper. None of this will be of much interest to anyone but me, and it is not my intention to make it otherwise. With this now said, I make no further apology, and I shall proceed as honestly and as truthfully as I possibly can."

August 26 1945

please, MEET my GRANDPARENTS:

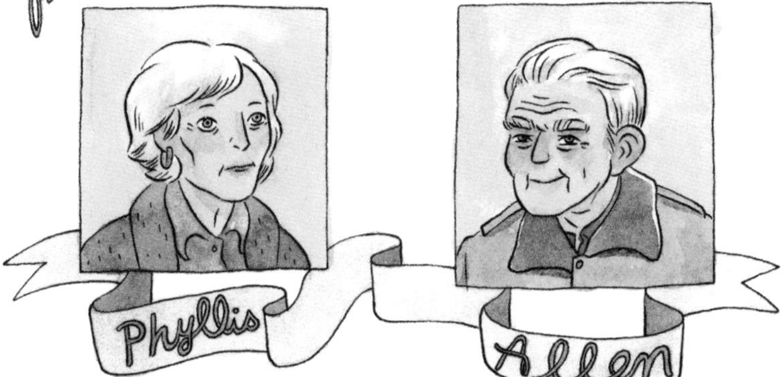

Phyllis
Allen

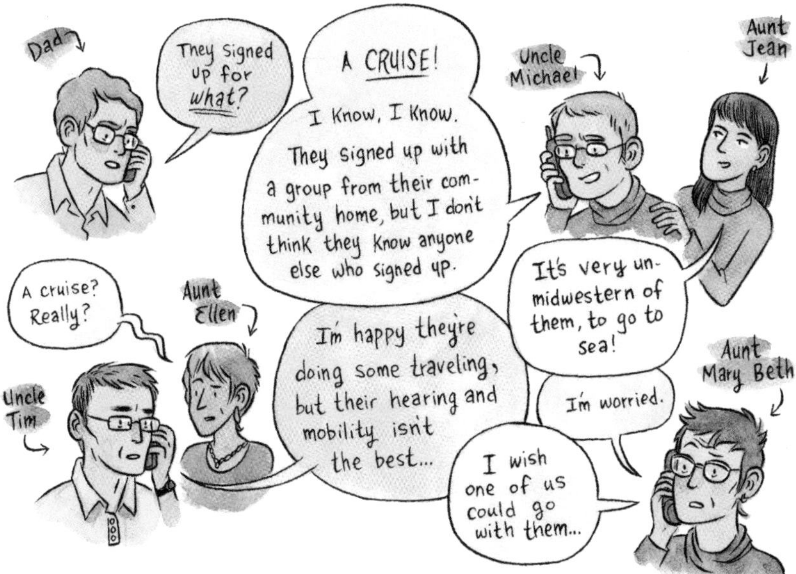

Dad
They signed up for what?
A CRUISE!
I know, I know. They signed up with a group from their community home, but I don't think they know anyone else who signed up.
Uncle Michael
Aunt Jean
It's very un-midwestern of them, to go to sea!
A cruise? Really?
Uncle Tim
Aunt Ellen
I'm happy they're doing some traveling, but their hearing and mobility isn't the best...
I'm worried.
Aunt Mary Beth
I wish one of us could go with them...

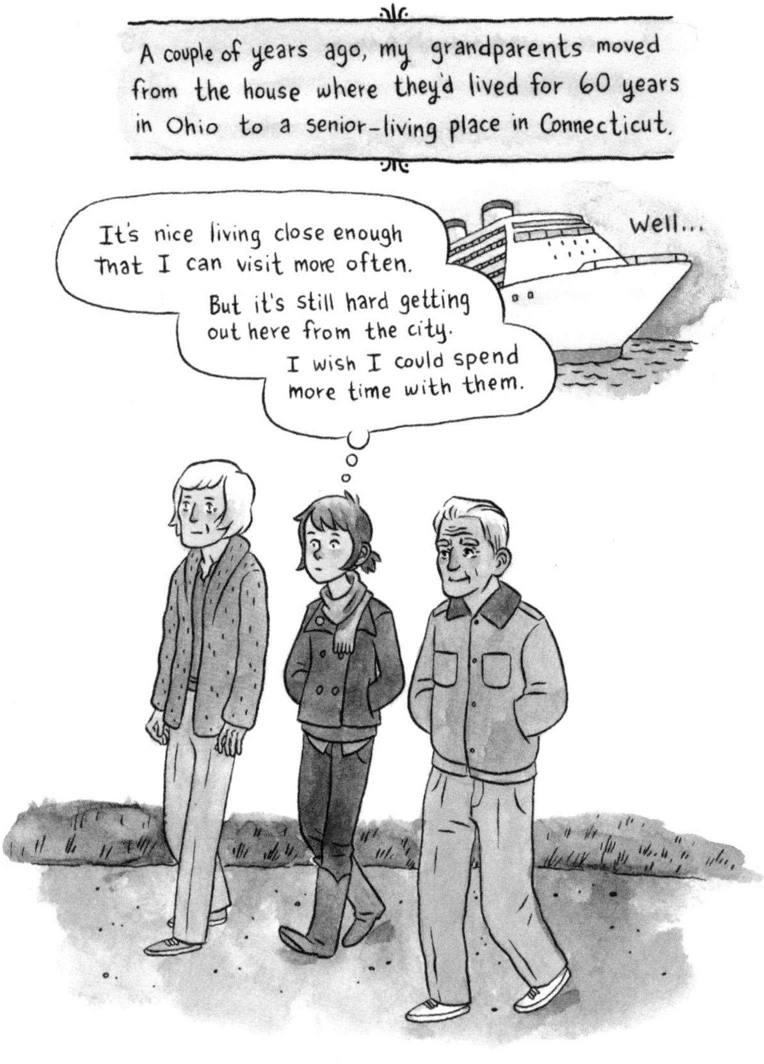
A couple of years ago, my grandparents moved from the house where they'd lived for 60 years in Ohio to a senior-living place in Connecticut.
It's nice living close enough that I can visit more often.
But it's still hard getting out here from the city.
I wish I could spend more time with them.
Well...

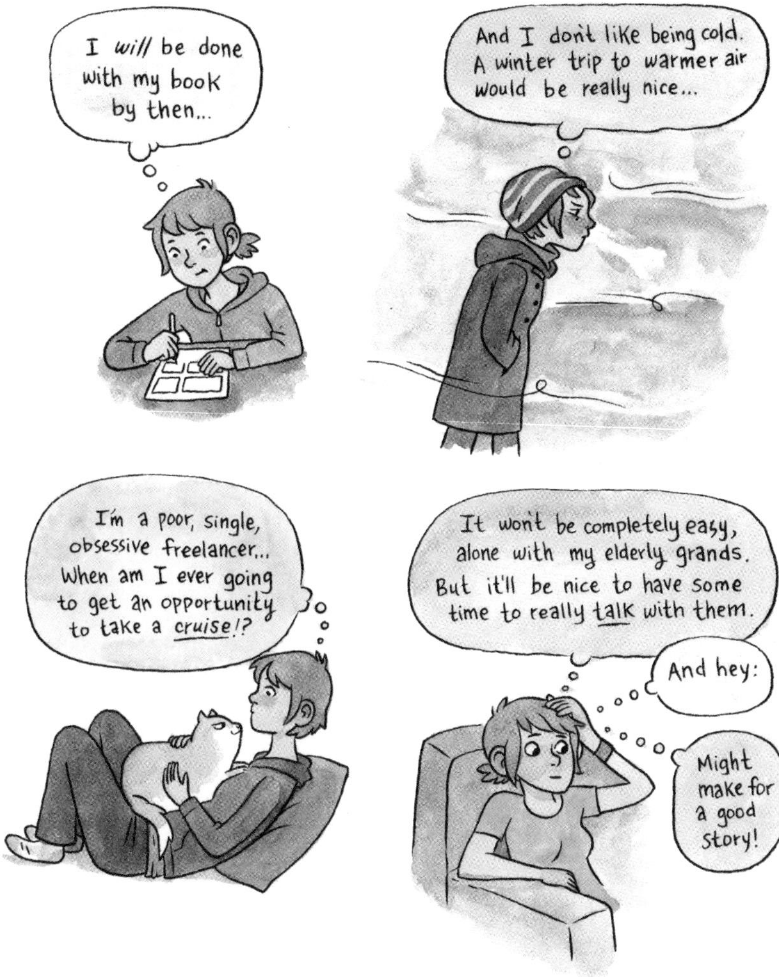
I *will* be done with my book by then...
And I don't like being cold. A winter trip to warmer air would be really nice...
I'm a poor, single, obsessive freelancer... When am I ever going to get an opportunity to take a cruise!?
It won't be completely easy, alone with my elderly grands. But it'll be nice to have some time to really talk with them.
And hey:
Might make for a good story!

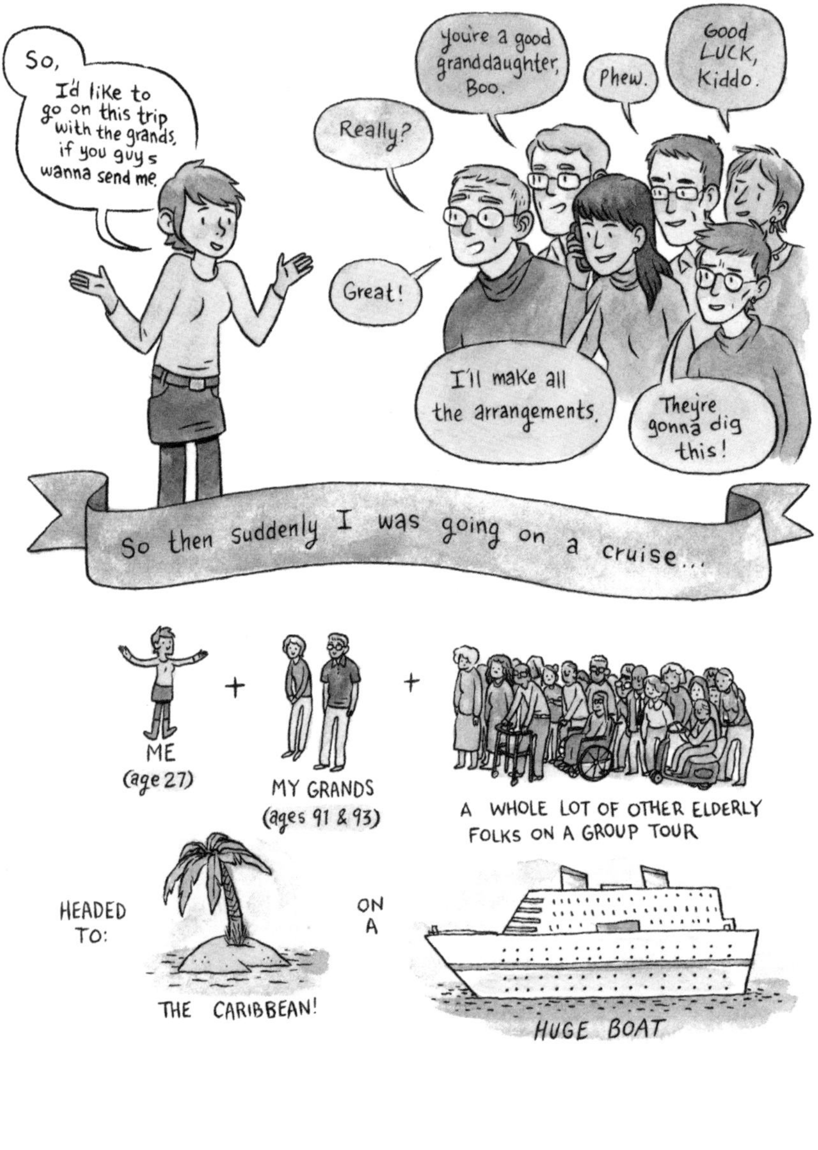
So, I'd like to go on this trip with the grands, if you guys wanna send me.
Really?
You're a good granddaughter, Boo.
Phew.
Good LUCK, Kiddo.
Great!
I'll make all the arrangements.
Theyre gonna dig this!
So then suddenly I was going on a cruise...
ME (age 27)
+
MY GRANDS (ages 91 & 93)
+
A WHOLE LOT OF OTHER ELDERLY FOLKS ON A GROUP TOUR
HEADED TO:
THE CARIBBEAN!
ON A
HUGE BOAT

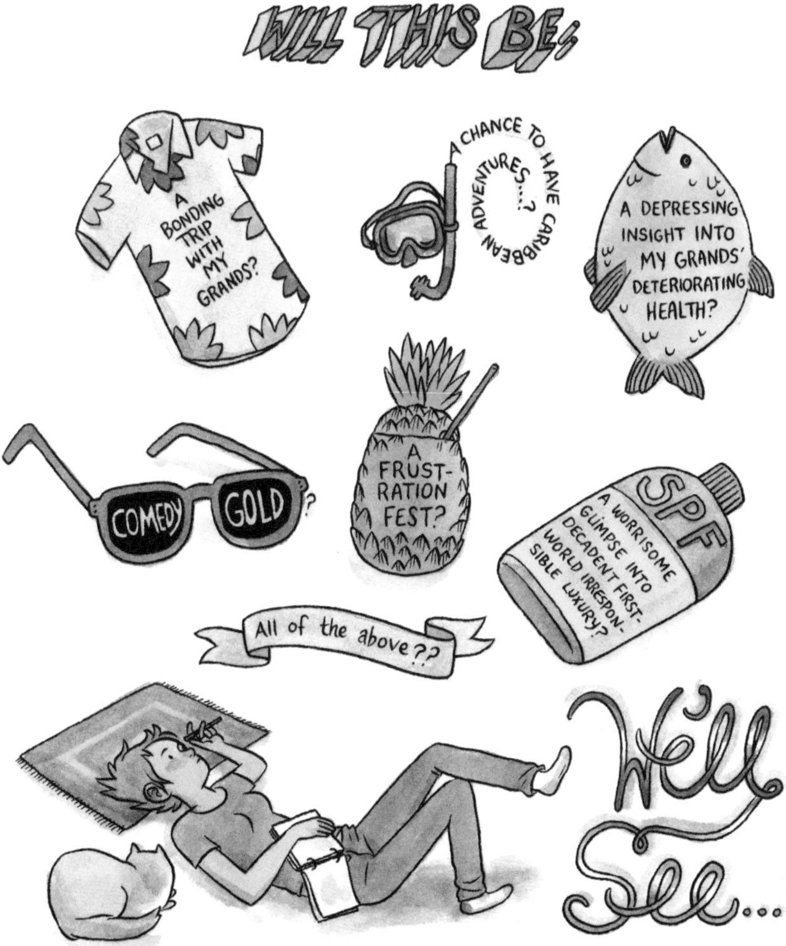
WILL THIS BE:
A BONDING TRIP WITH MY GRANDS?
A CHANCE TO HAVE CARIBBEAN ADVENTURES...?
A DEPRESSING INSIGHT INTO MY GRANDS' DETERIORATING HEALTH?
COMEDY GOLD?
A FRUST-RATION FEST?
A WORRISOME GLIMPSE INTO DECADENT FIRST-WORLD IRRESPON-SIBLE LUXURY?
SPF
All of the above??
We'll see...

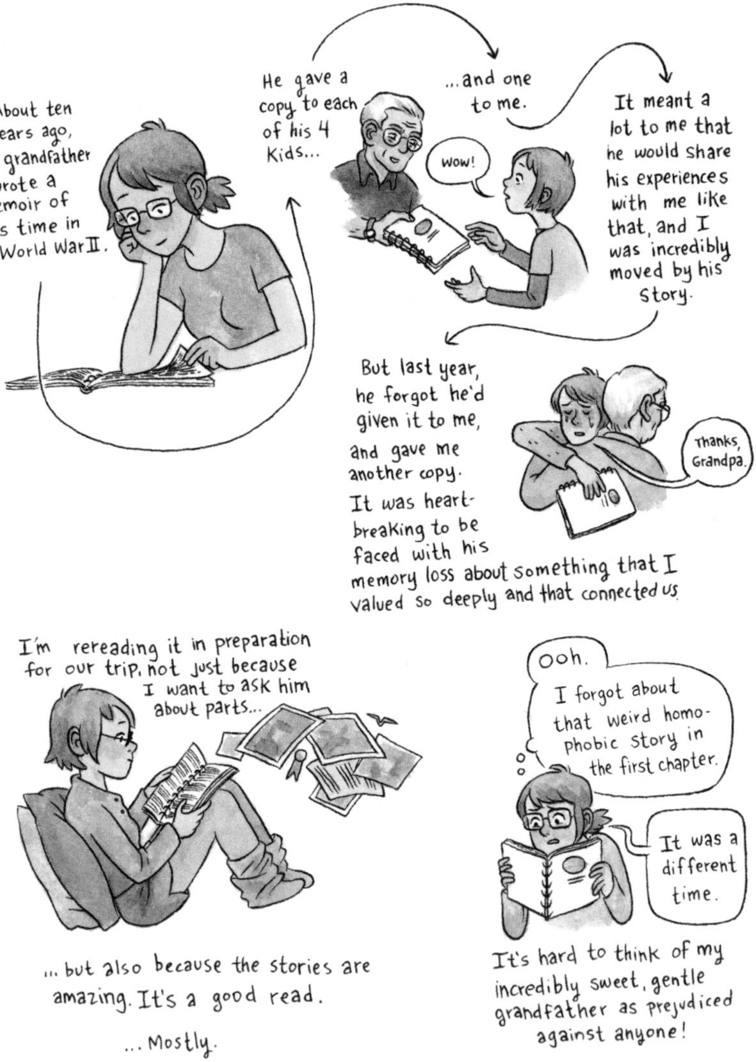
About ten years ago, my grandfather wrote a memoir of his time in World War II.
He gave a copy to each of his 4 Kids...
...and one to me.
Wow!
It meant a lot to me that he would share his experiences with me like that, and I was incredibly moved by his story.
But last year, he forgot he'd given it to me, and gave me another copy.
Thanks, Grandpa.
It was heart-breaking to be faced with his memory loss about something that I valued so deeply and that connected us.
I'm rereading it in preparation for our trip, not just because I want to ask him about parts...
...but also because the stories are amazing. It's a good read.
...Mostly.
Ooh. I forgot about that weird homo-phobic story in the first chapter.
It was a different time.
It's hard to think of my incredibly sweet, gentle grandfather as prejudiced against anyone!

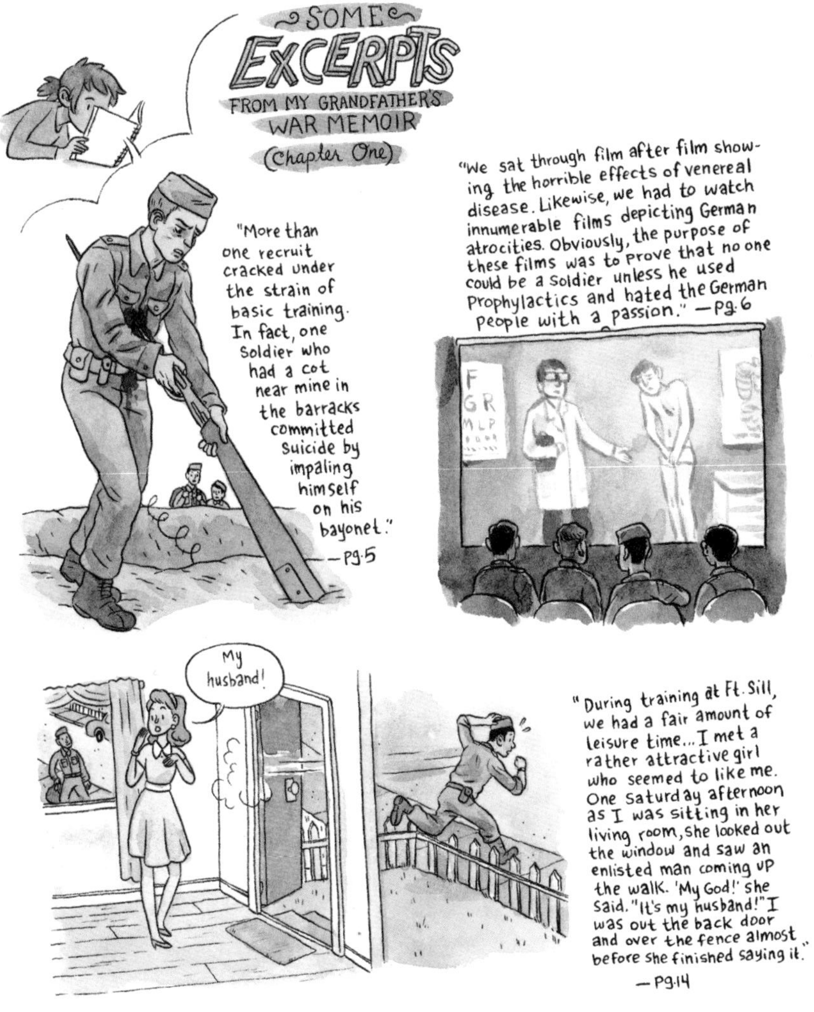
SOME EXCERPTS FROM MY GRANDFATHER'S WAR MEMOIR
(Chapter One)
"More than one recruit cracked under the strain of basic training. In fact, one soldier who had a cot near mine in the barracks committed suicide by impaling himself on his bayonet." —Pg.5
"We sat through film after film showing the horrible effects of venereal disease. Likewise, we had to watch innumerable films depicting German atrocities. Obviously, the purpose of these films was to prove that no one could be a soldier unless he used prophylactics and hated the German people with a passion." —Pg.6
F
G R
M L P
My husband!
"During training at Ft. Sill, we had a fair amount of leisure time... I met a rather attractive girl who seemed to like me. One saturday afternoon as I was sitting in her living room, she looked out the window and saw an enlisted man coming up the walk. 'My God!' she said. "It's my husband!" I was out the back door and over the fence almost before she finished saying it."
—Pg.14

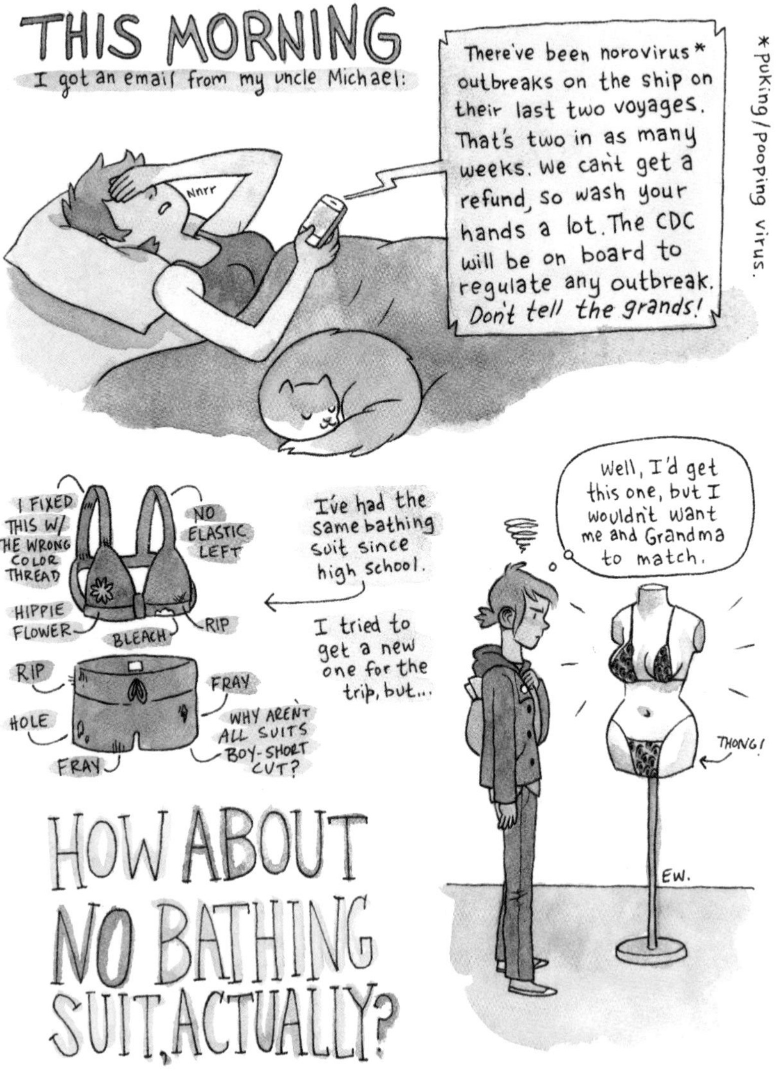
THIS MORNING
I got an email from my uncle Michael:
Nnrr
There've been norovirus* outbreaks on the ship on their last two voyages. That's two in as many weeks. We can't get a refund, so wash your hands a lot. The CDC will be on board to regulate any outbreak. Don't tell the grands!
*Puking/Pooping virus.
I FIXED THIS W/ THE WRONG COLOR THREAD
NO ELASTIC LEFT
HIPPIE FLOWER
BLEACH
RIP
RIP
FRAY
HOLE
FRAY
WHY AREN'T ALL SUITS BOY-SHORT CUT?
I've had the same bathing suit since high school.
I tried to get a new one for the trip, but...
Well, I'd get this one, but I wouldn't want me and Grandma to match.
THONG!
EW.
HOW ABOUT NO BATHING SUIT, ACTUALLY?

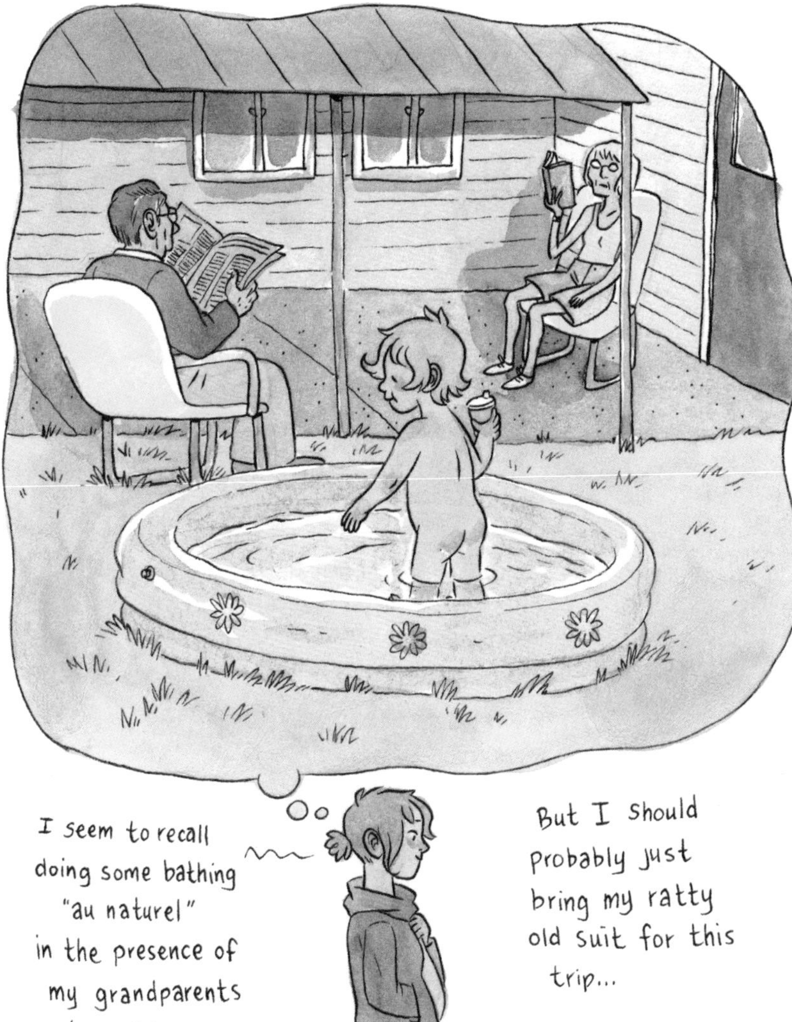
I seem to recall doing some bathing "au naturel" in the presence of my grandparents long ago...
But I should probably just bring my ratty old suit for this trip...

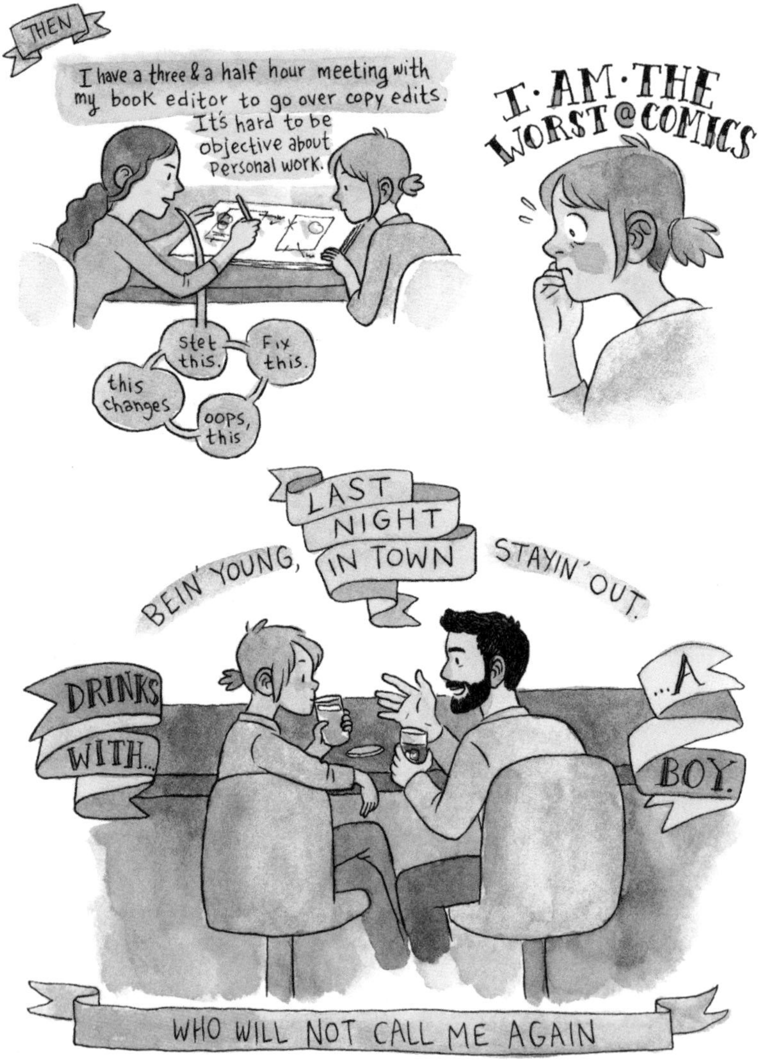
THEN
I have a three & a half hour meeting with my book editor to go over copy edits.
It's hard to be objective about personal work.
stet this.
Fix this.
this changes
oops, this
I·AM·THE WORST@COMICS
LAST NIGHT IN TOWN
BEIN' YOUNG,
STAYIN' OUT.
DRINKS WITH...
...A BOY.
WHO WILL NOT CALL ME AGAIN

Day 1

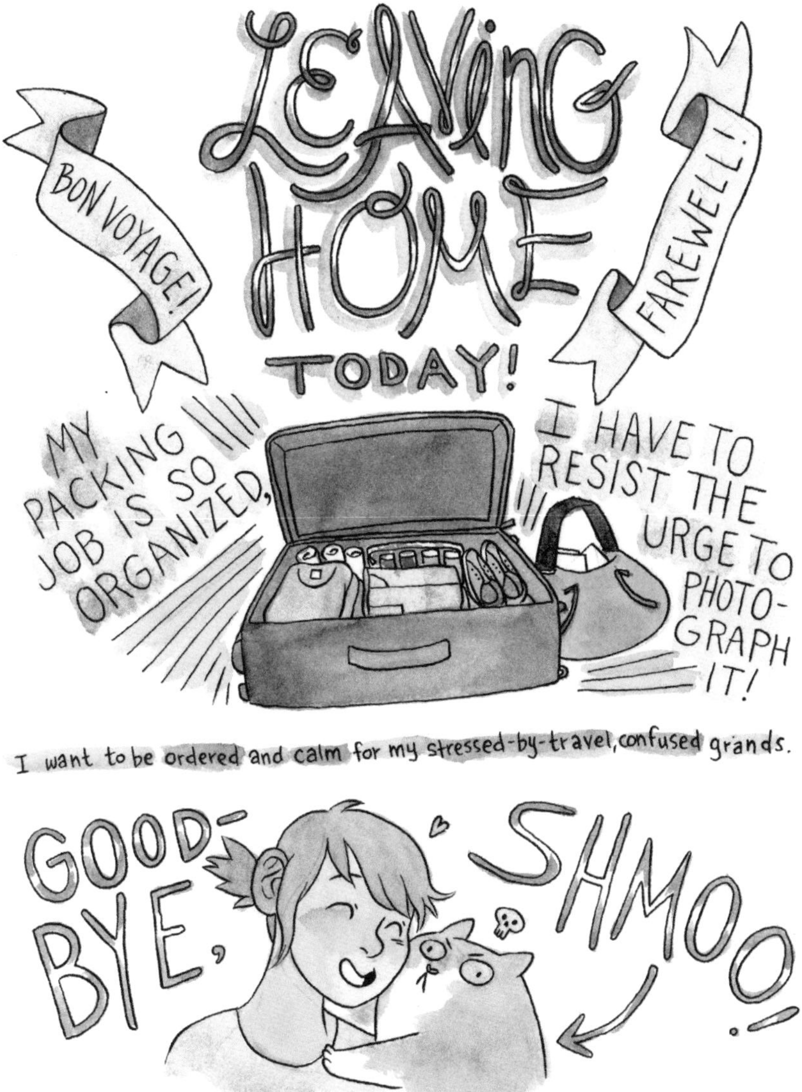
LEAVING HOME TODAY!
BON VOYAGE!
FAREWELL!
MY PACKING JOB IS SO ORGANIZED,
I HAVE TO RESIST THE URGE TO PHOTOGRAPH IT!
I want to be ordered and calm for my stressed-by-travel, confused grands.
GOOD-BYE, SHMOO!

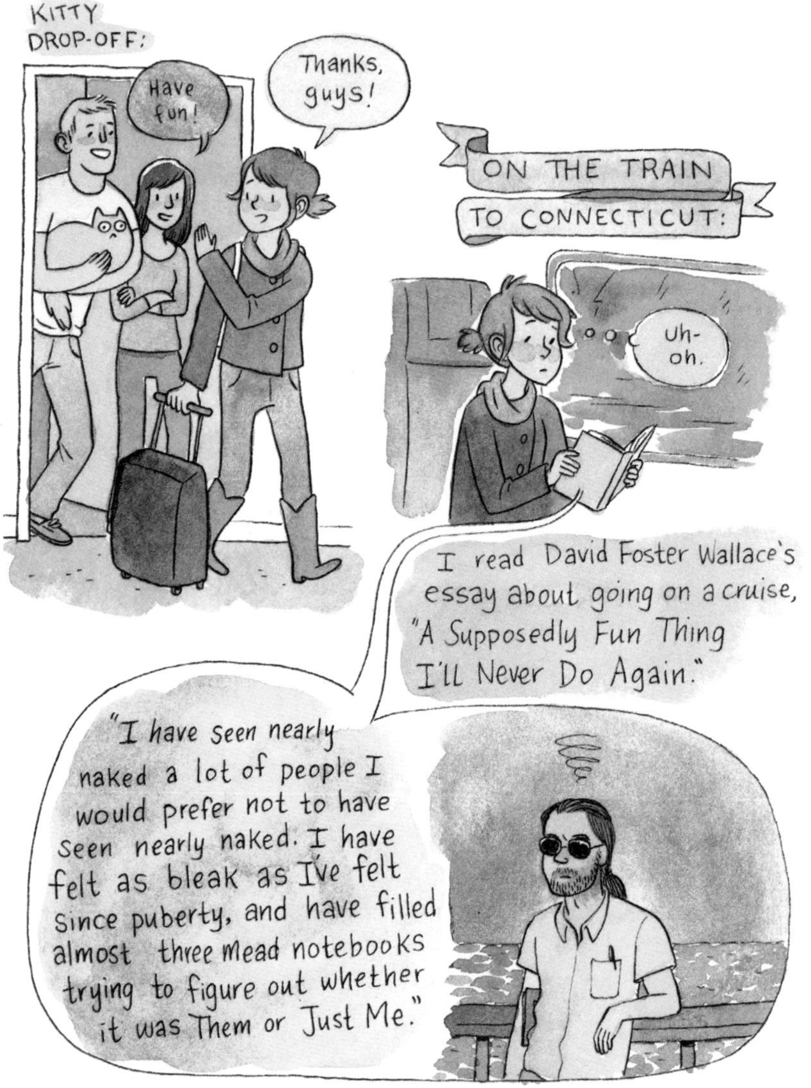
KITTY DROP-OFF:
Have fun!
Thanks, guys!
ON THE TRAIN TO CONNECTICUT:
Uh-oh.
I read David Foster Wallace's essay about going on a cruise, "A Supposedly Fun Thing I'll Never Do Again."
"I have seen nearly naked a lot of people I would prefer not to have seen nearly naked. I have felt as bleak as I've felt since puberty, and have filled almost three mead notebooks trying to figure out whether it was Them or Just Me."

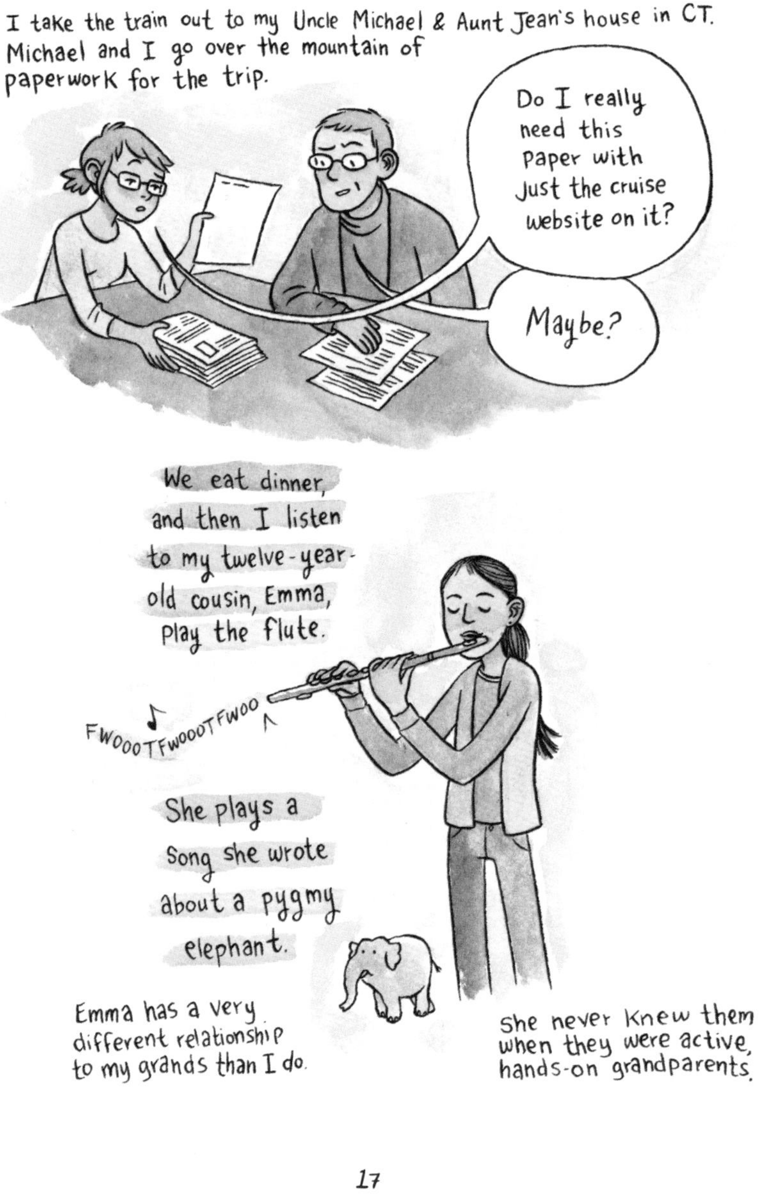
I take the train out to my Uncle Michael & Aunt Jean's house in CT. Michael and I go over the mountain of paperwork for the trip.
Do I really need this paper with just the cruise website on it?
Maybe?
We eat dinner, and then I listen to my twelve-year-old cousin, Emma, play the flute.
FWOOOTFWOOOTFWOO
She plays a song she wrote about a pygmy elephant.
Emma has a very different relationship to my grands than I do.
She never knew them when they were active, hands-on grandparents.

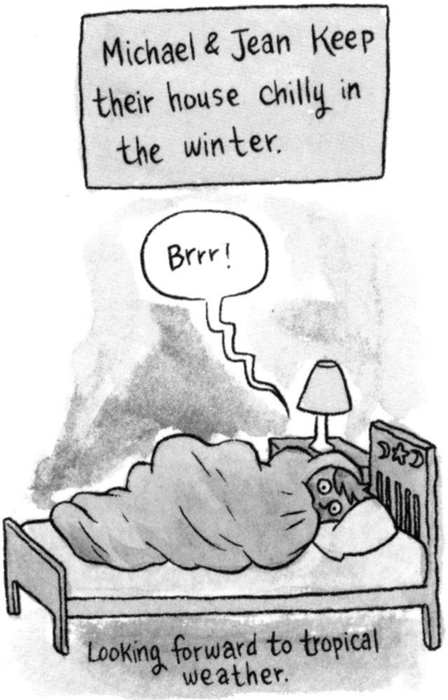
Michael & Jean Keep their house chilly in the winter.
Brrr!
Looking forward to tropical weather.

"I solo (flew) after about nine hours. I'll never forget that day! I was practicing landings and takeoffs, and Mr. Jarrard seemed very unhappy with my performance. As we taxied back and got set for another takeoff, he suddenly opened the door, and as he climbed out he said, 'Hell, you're gonna get me killed! I'm getting out. You go on yourself.' A great way to inspire confidence in a student." —pg. 11

"Soon after I'd soloed, I was flying a rectangle pattern, when during a steep bank, the door on the downside suddenly popped open and I was looking at nothing but the ground." —pg. 11

Day 2

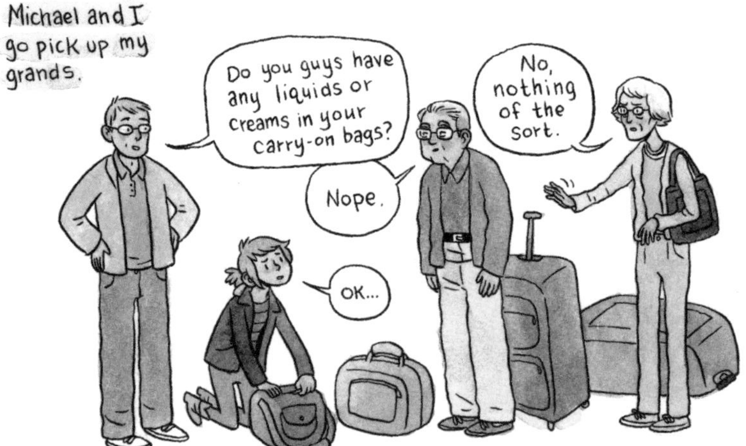
Michael and I go pick up my grands.
Do you guys have any liquids or creams in your carry-on bags?
Nope.
OK...
No, nothing of the sort.

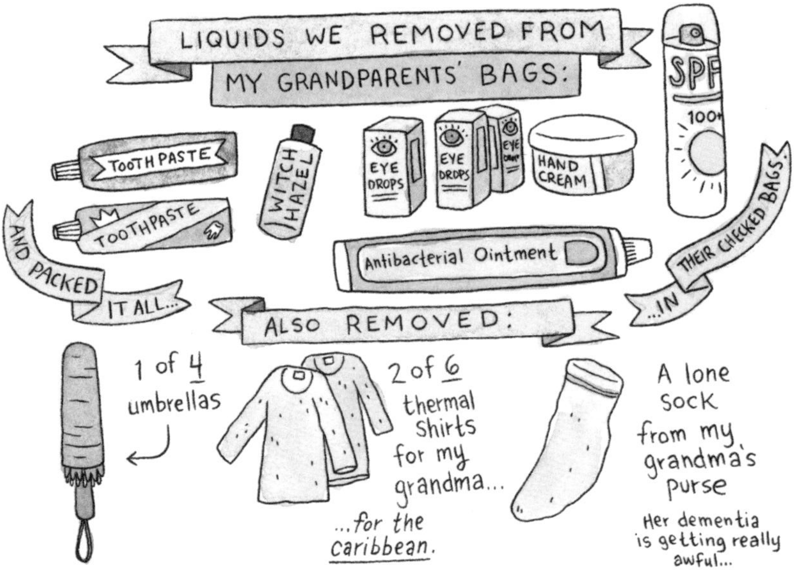
LIQUIDS WE REMOVED FROM MY GRANDPARENTS' BAGS:
TOOTHPASTE
TOOTHPASTE
WITCH HAZEL
EYE DROPS
EYE DROPS
EYE
HAND CREAM
SPF
100+
Antibacterial Ointment
AND PACKED IT ALL...
...IN THEIR CHECKED BAGS.
ALSO REMOVED:
1 of 4 umbrellas
2 of 6 thermal shirts for my grandma...
...for the caribbean.
A lone sock from my grandma's purse
Her dementia is getting really awful...

Frankly, my grandparents' mental and physical health has declined rapidly since their move from their old home.

I still think of them as quiet, scholarly retired schoolteachers, with the capabilities of five years previous, so every time I see them I am newly horrified and shocked by their decline.

Conversation is difficult for them (not that my family are big talkers).

And my grandma isn't really aware of where she is or who anyone is (besides my grandpa).

Mostly she calls me "Jean."

My grandpa is a bit better, but he can't see or hear or walk well.

Well, I'm not sure who this is, but I suppose I'm going with, um, to... the... uh...

Hm?

They're stubborn about help, though- stoic and uncomplaining.

Thank god they have each other.

Married for 67 years, they're practically a single organism.

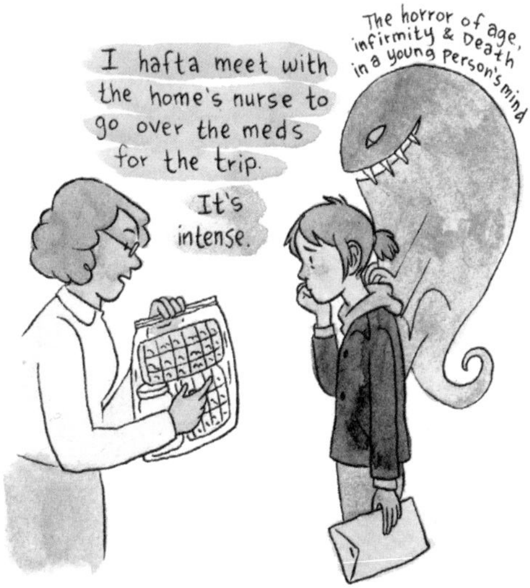
I hafta meet with the home's nurse to go over the meds for the trip.
It's intense.
The horror of age, infirmity & Death in a young person's mind

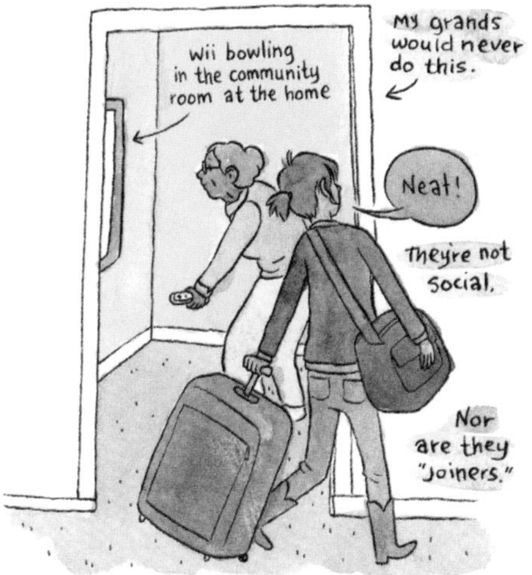
Wii bowling in the community room at the home
My grands would never do this.
Neat!
They're not social.
Nor are they "joiners."

I'm usually an

Airport Ninja

No metal →

← Gets through Security like a Pro

No liquids ↘

Super fast walker

Slip-on Shoes

Not so Much this time

The less said about our trip through security, the absolute better.

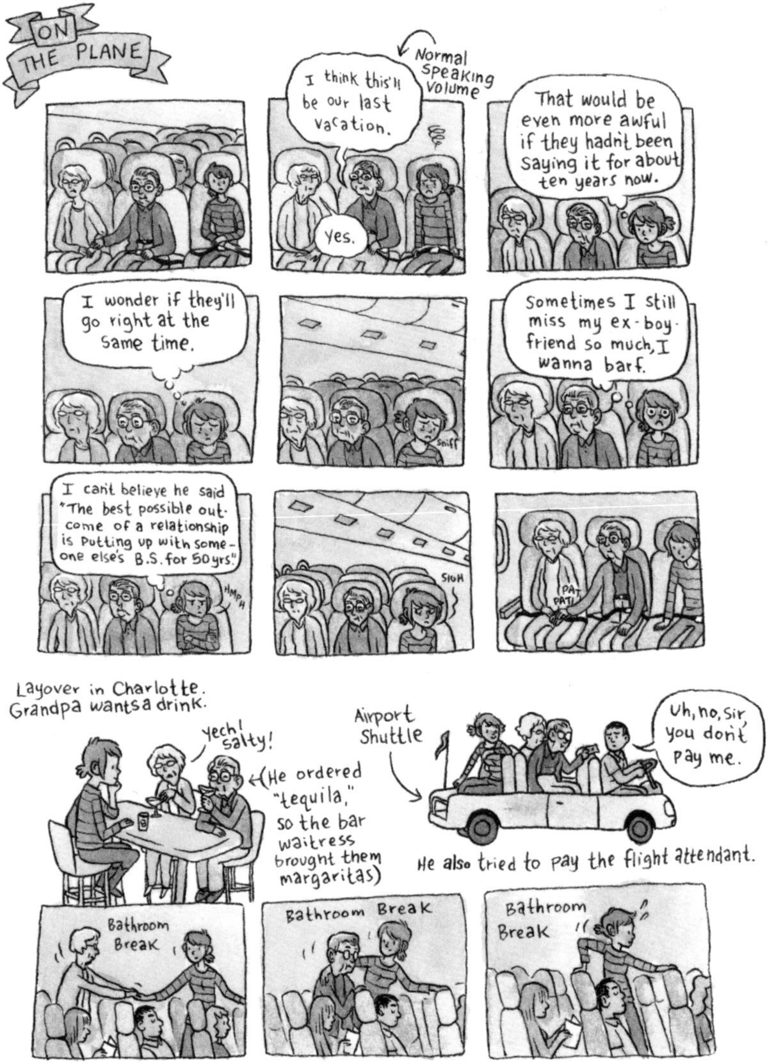

ON THE PLANE
I think this'll be our last vacation.
Normal speaking volume
Yes.
That would be even more awful if they hadn't been saying it for about ten years now.
I wonder if they'll go right at the same time.
SNIFF
Sometimes I still miss my ex-boyfriend so much, I wanna barf.
I can't believe he said "The best possible outcome of a relationship is putting up with someone else's B.S. for 50 yrs."
HMPH
SIGH
PAT PAT
Layover in Charlotte. Grandpa wants a drink.
Yech! Salty!
(He ordered "tequila," so the bar waitress brought them margaritas)
Airport Shuttle
Uh, no, sir, you don't pay me.
He also tried to pay the flight attendant.
Bathroom Break
Bathroom Break
Bathroom Break

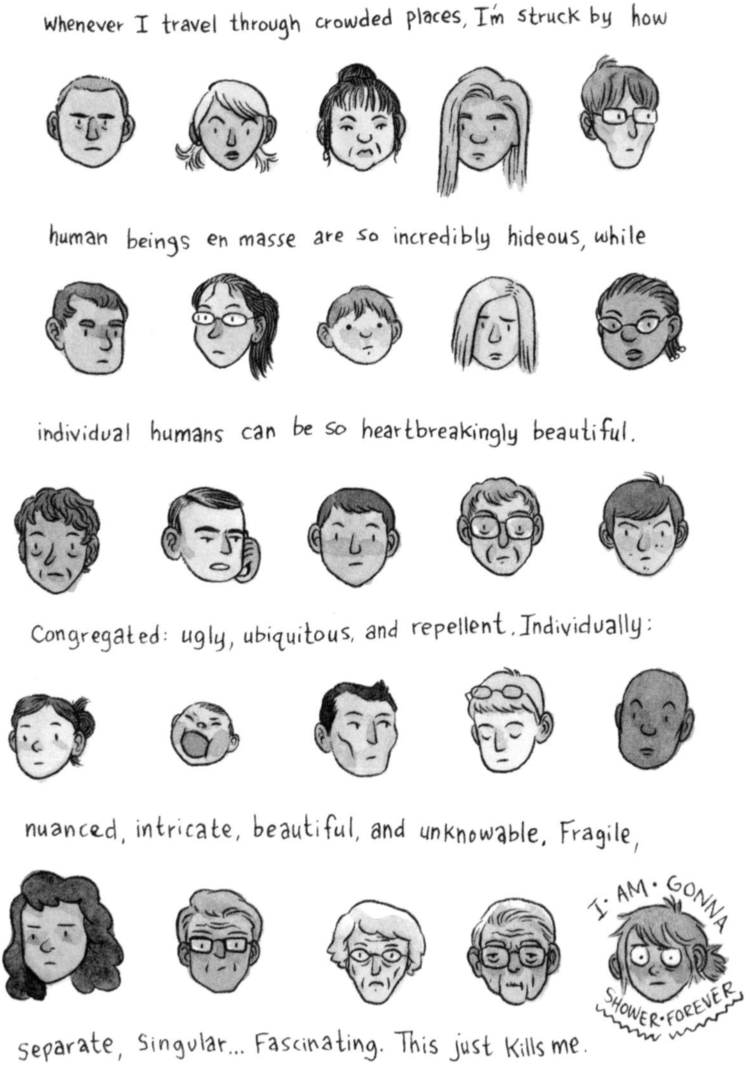
Whenever I travel through crowded places, I'm struck by how
human beings en masse are so incredibly hideous, while
individual humans can be so heartbreakingly beautiful.
Congregated: ugly, ubiquitous, and repellent. Individually:
nuanced, intricate, beautiful, and unknowable. Fragile,
I · AM · GONNA SHOWER · FOREVER
separate, singular... Fascinating. This just kills me.

While waiting for our bags at baggage claim, Grandpa has his second accident of the (very long) day.

FUCK YOU, YOU STUPID A-HOLE!

SOMEDAY YOU'LL BE AN OLD MAN PISSING YOUR PANTS, AND I'LL MAKE THAT FUCKING FACE AT YOU!

STOP LOOKING AT MY GRANDPA LIKE THAT, YOU TOTAL SHIT!

I wasn't really prepared for this aspect of our trip, and I'm not sure how to handle it.

Grandpa doesn't seem bothered or all that aware of his situation, but passersby are.

29

Seriously!?

We're the only ones on the hotel shuttle bus, so when the driver lets us off across the street from the hotel & won't help with the bags, I start to lose it.

OK, hurry! There's no crosswalk!

Hotel room service

Water, Grandma?

Wanna change your pants Grandpa?

No.

Well, I suppose so...

No shower...

Has ever felt better...

...than this shower.

♥ AT LAST ♥

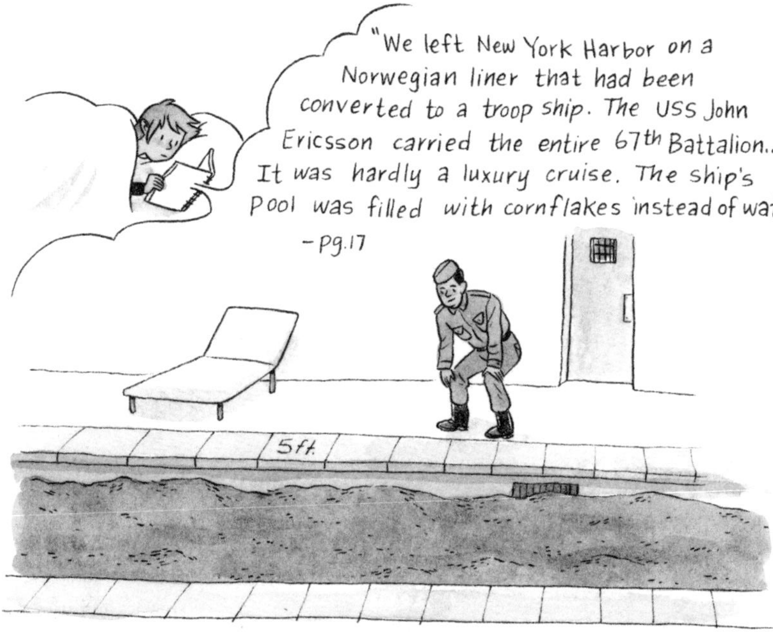
"We left New York Harbor on a Norwegian liner that had been converted to a troop ship. The USS John Ericsson carried the entire 67th Battalion... It was hardly a luxury cruise. The ship's pool was filled with cornflakes instead of water." -pg.17
5ft.

"[I was stationed in Warminster.] Because the Salisbury Plain gave the division ample room for training, I practiced landings and takeoffs from many different spots. The famous Stonehenge monument at that time was not commercialized or protected by fences. Thus I could land and taxi right up to it!" -pg.19

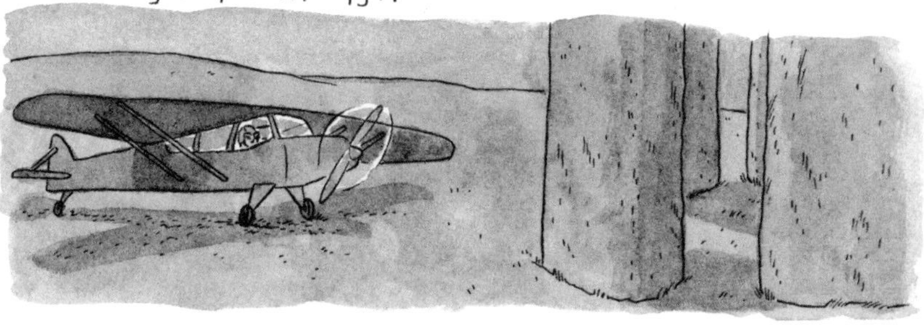

Day 3

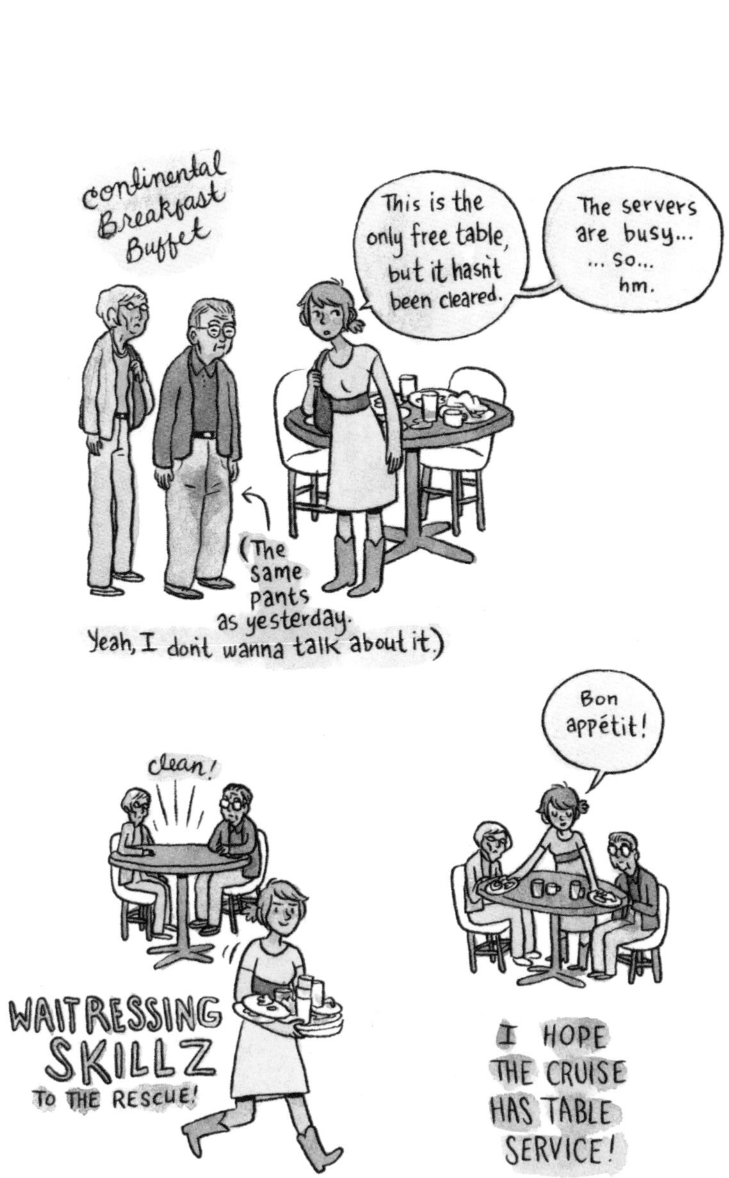
Continental Breakfast Buffet
This is the only free table, but it hasn't been cleared.
The servers are busy... ... so... hm.
(The same pants as yesterday. Yeah, I don't wanna talk about it.)
clean!
WAITRESSING SKILLZ TO THE RESCUE!
Bon appétit!
I HOPE THE CRUISE HAS TABLE SERVICE!

We take a little walk through the scenic parking lots of Ft. Lauderdale.

Click

THE LOBBY PRE-BOARDING

IS ABSOLUTE CHAOS!

MY DOCTOR SAYS I'M IN THE EARLY STAGES OF FOSSILIZATION

NATURE

Thinking unkind thoughts →

← Feeling guilty

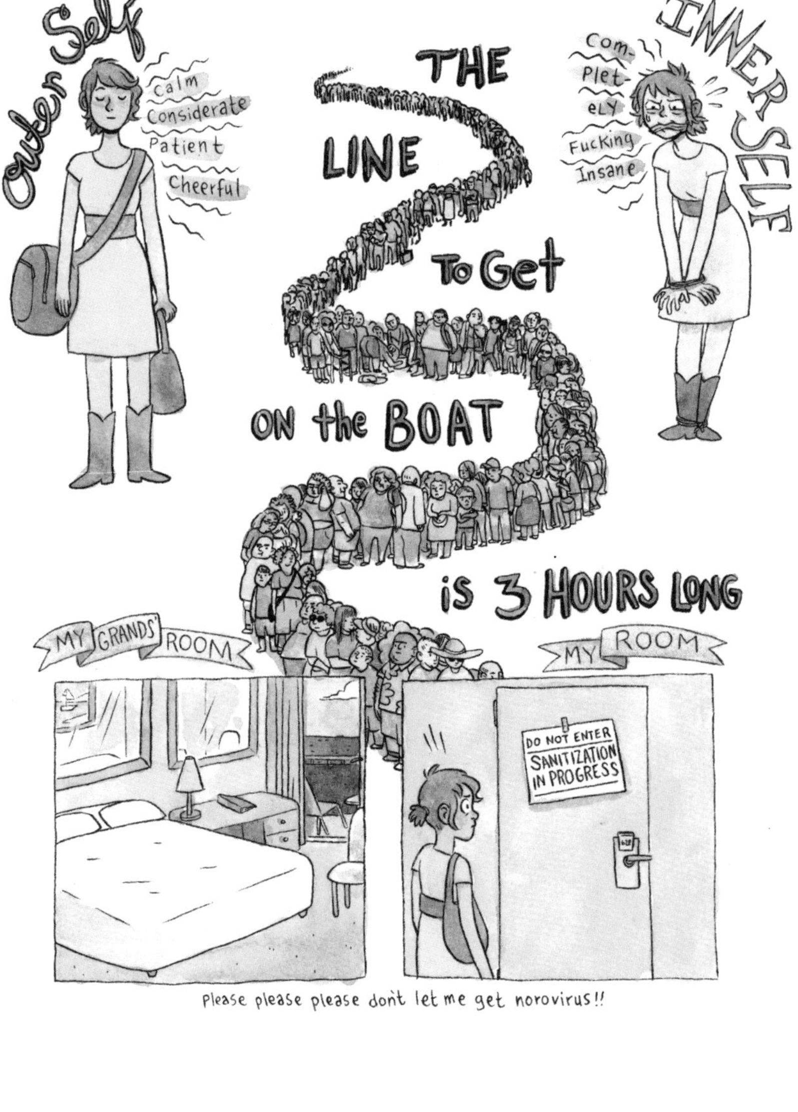
Outer Self
Calm
Considerate
Patient
Cheerful
THE LINE To Get ON the BOAT is 3 HOURS LONG
INNER SELF
Com-plet-eLY Fucking Insane
MY GRANDS' ROOM
MY ROOM
DO NOT ENTER
SANITIZATION IN PROGRESS

Please please please don't let me get norovirus!!

There are 4,700 people on board this insane floating city! It's enormous and confusing and where the hell are we?

But I pretend to know the way, and my grandparents follow.

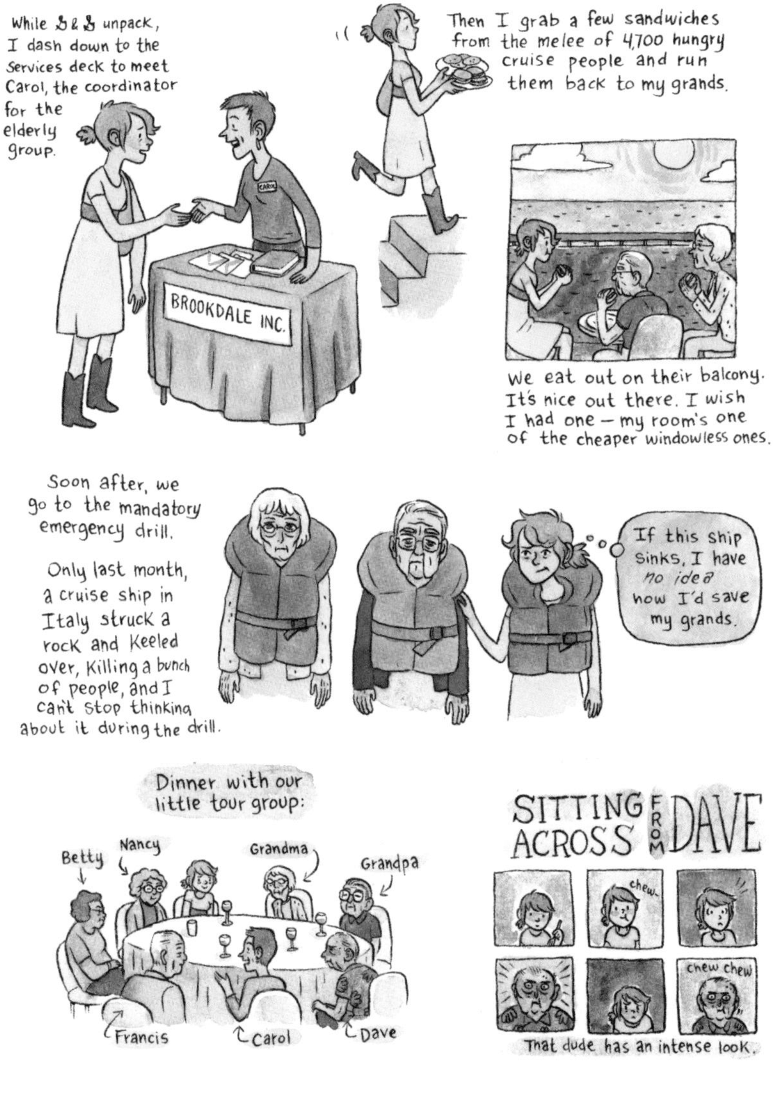

While G & G unpack, I dash down to the services deck to meet Carol, the coordinator for the elderly group.
CAROL
BROOKDALE INC.
Then I grab a few sandwiches from the melee of 4,700 hungry cruise people and run them back to my grands.
We eat out on their balcony. It's nice out there. I wish I had one — my room's one of the cheaper windowless ones.
Soon after, we go to the mandatory emergency drill.
Only last month, a cruise ship in Italy struck a rock and keeled over, killing a bunch of people, and I can't stop thinking about it during the drill.
If this ship sinks, I have no idea how I'd save my grands.
Dinner with our little tour group:
Betty
Nancy
Grandma
Grandpa
Francis
Carol
Dave
SITTING ACROSS FROM DAVE
chew
chew chew
That dude has an intense look.

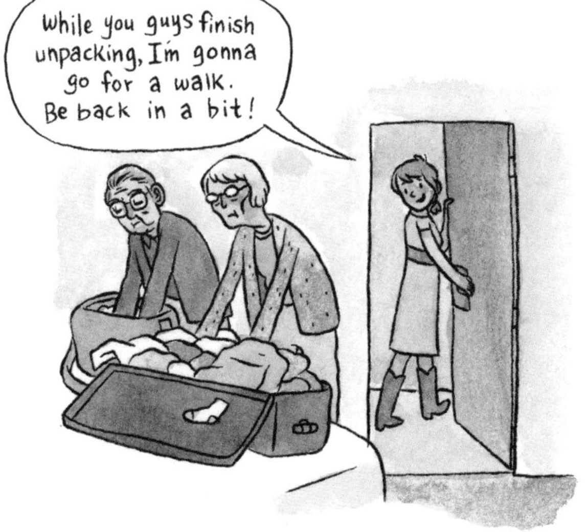
While you guys finish unpacking, I'm gonna go for a walk. Be back in a bit!

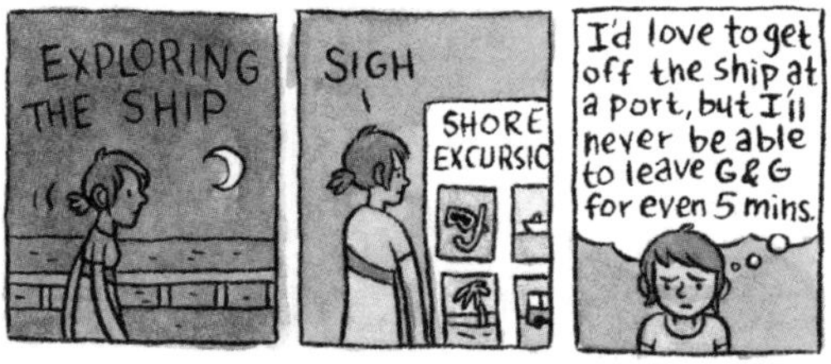
EXPLORING THE SHIP
SIGH
SHORE
EXCURSIO
I'd love to get off the ship at a port, but I'll never be able to leave G&G for even 5 mins.

In a fit of rebellion,
I sign up for a snorkeling excursion.

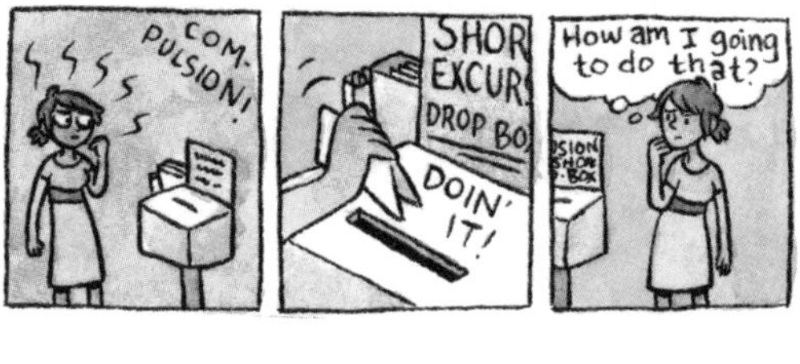
COM-PULSION!
SHOR
EXCURS
DROP BO
DOIN' IT!
How am I going to do that?

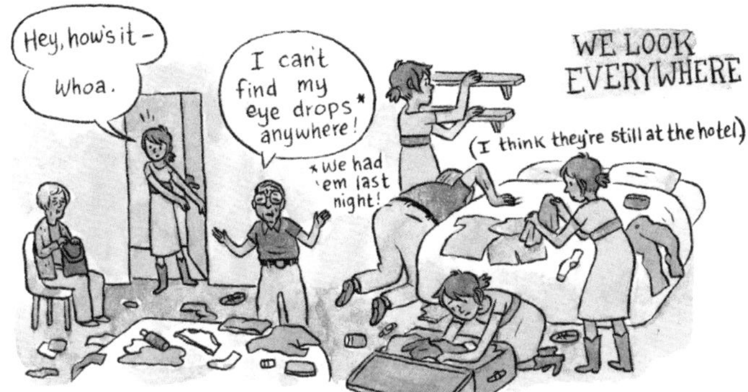
Hey, how's it -
Whoa.
I can't find my eye drops* anywhere!
*we had 'em last night!
WE LOOK EVERYWHERE
(I think they're still at the hotel)

My grandma's packing situation is way worse than I thought.
It looks like she just emptied cabinets into her suitcase.

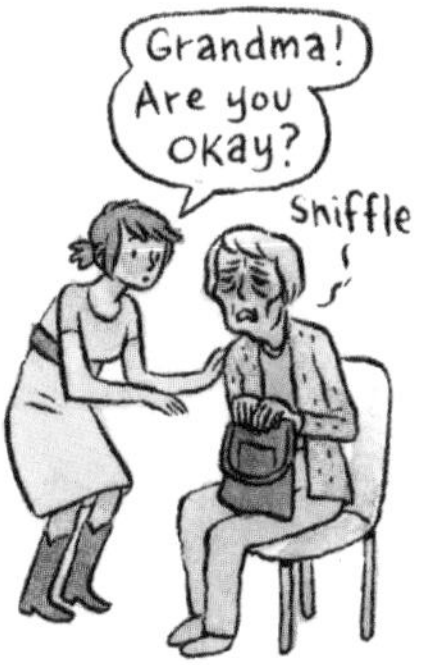
Grandma! Are you okay?
Sniffle

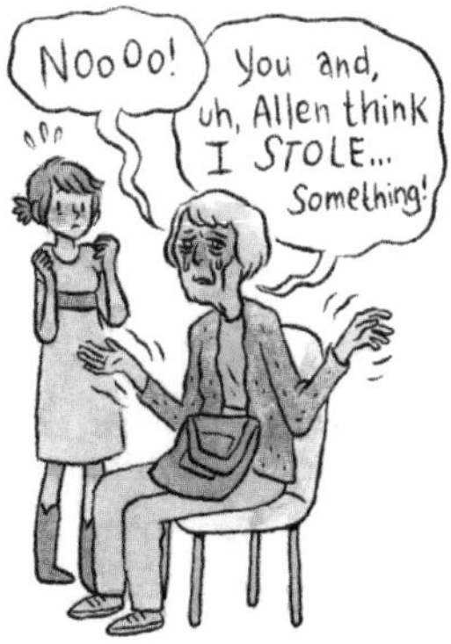
NooOo!
You and, uh, Allen think I STOLE... Something!

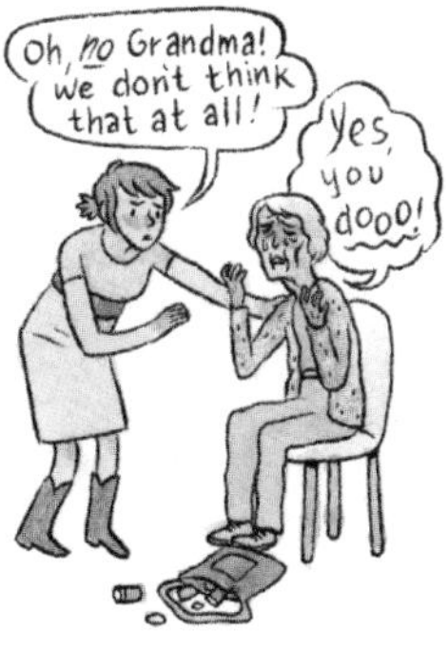
Oh, no Grandma! We don't think that at all!
Yes, you dooo!

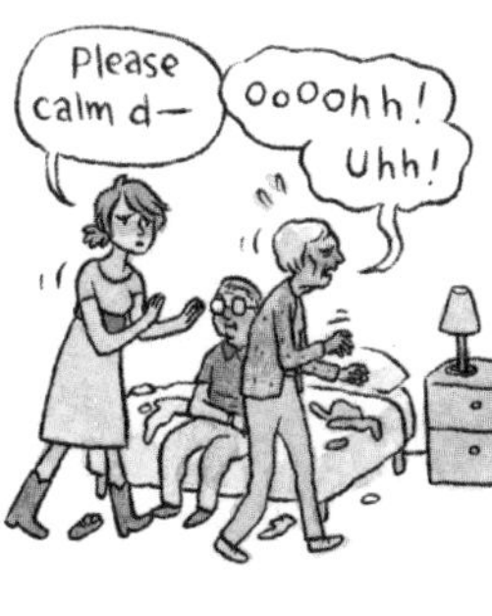
Please calm d—
OoOohh! Uhh!

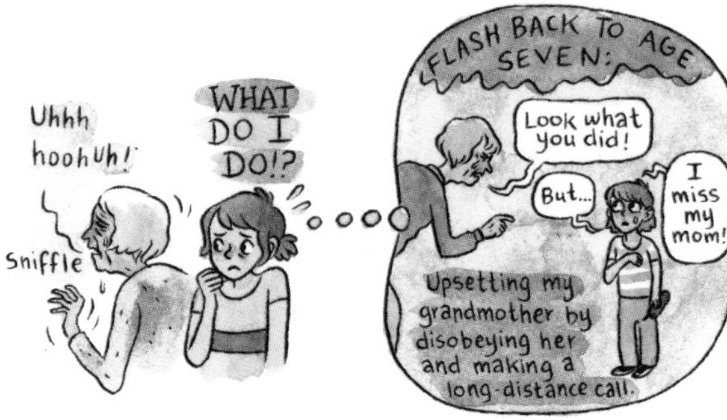
Uhhh hoohuh!
sniffle
WHAT DO I DO!?
FLASH BACK TO AGE SEVEN:
Look what you did!
But...
I miss my mom!
Upsetting my grandmother by disobeying her and making a long-distance call.

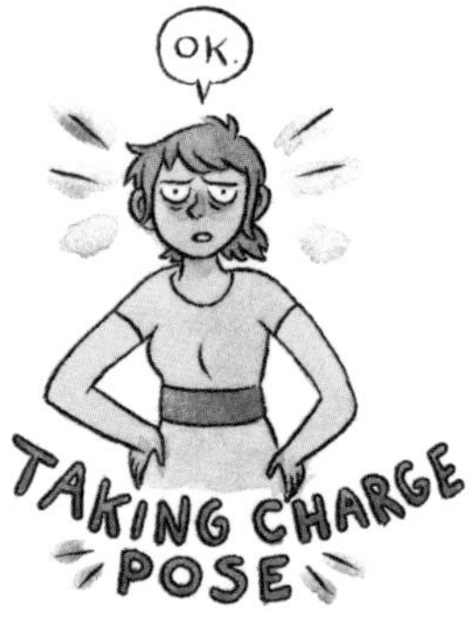
OK.
TAKING CHARGE POSE

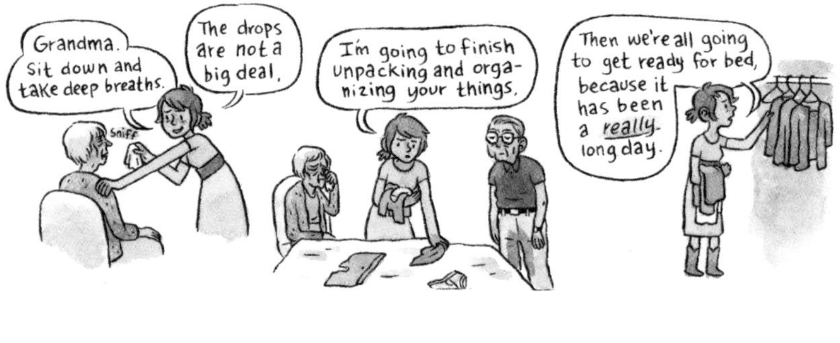
Grandma. Sit down and take deep breaths.
Sniff
The drops are not a big deal.
I'm going to finish unpacking and organizing your things.
Then we're all going to get ready for bed, because it has been a really long day.

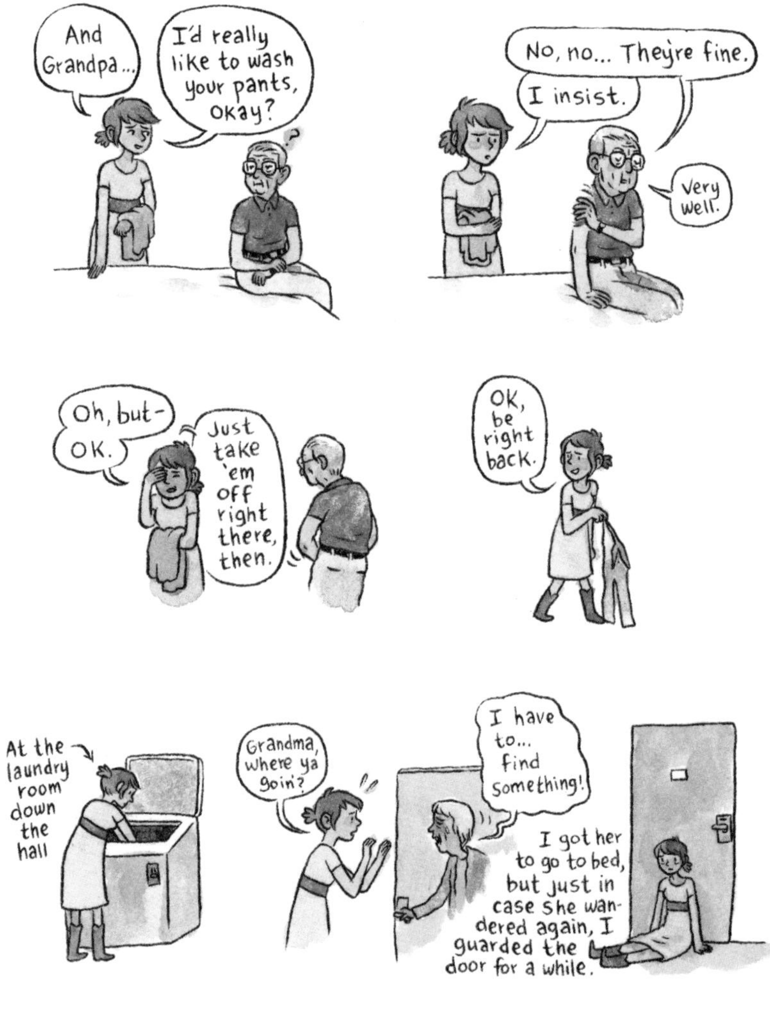
And Grandpa...
I'd really like to wash your pants, okay?
?
No, no... They're fine.
I insist.
Very well.
Oh, but- OK.
Just take 'em off right there, then.
OK, be right back.
At the laundry room down the hall
Grandma, where ya goin'?
I have to... find something!
I got her to go to bed, but just in case she wandered again, I guarded the door for a while.

BACK
IN MY OWN
ROOM:

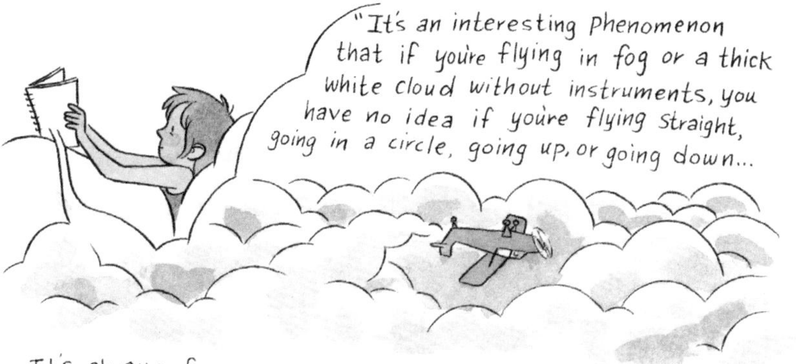
"It's an interesting phenomenon that if you're flying in fog or a thick white cloud without instruments, you have no idea if you're flying straight, going in a circle, going up, or going down...

...It's always fascinated me that if a person is a passenger in a light plane and has his eyes closed during a perfect loop, he will never know that he's been upside down. Centrifugal force keeps him pressed against the seat. I've done many a loop without fastening my seat belt, although I'm sure it's not a smart thing to do. This is called 'flying by the seat of your pants.'" -pg. 21

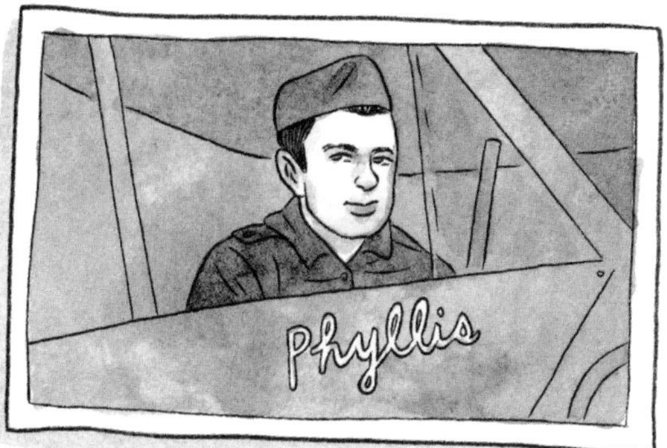
Phyllis

Grandpa in his Piper Cub plane, which he flew as a Spearhead Scout pilot. He also never wore a parachute, as they were "a bit uncomfortable."

I can't sleep.

I'd go get a drink at one of the *many* bars...

But the only thing sadder than being in this room right now is being at one of those bars, drinking alone.

I spent the last two days thinking about my grands and their needs...

...And now I can't turn it off.

How do people do this full time?

Oh god, please let it get easier on them tomorrow.

What are we doing here?! This is so far beyond their capabilities.

But it would have been awful to tell them they couldn't go.

OK. Clear your mind, Lucy.

But when I clear my mind, I'm just a person awake on a bed in the ocean...

...very, very alone.

Day 4

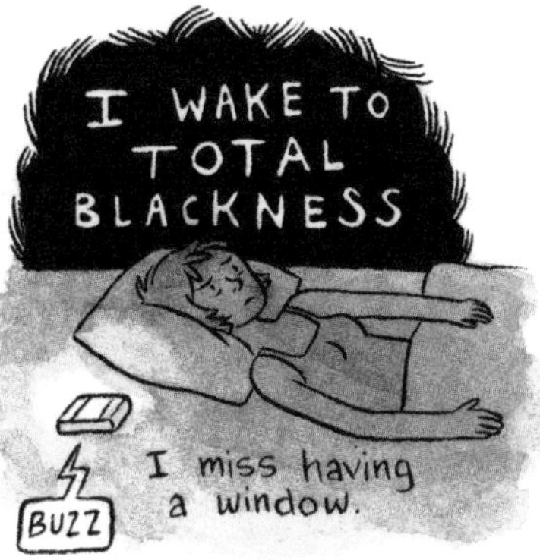
I WAKE TO TOTAL BLACKNESS
BUZZ
I miss having a window.

I have breakfast delivered to my grands' room, so we can eat on their balcony watching the waves.

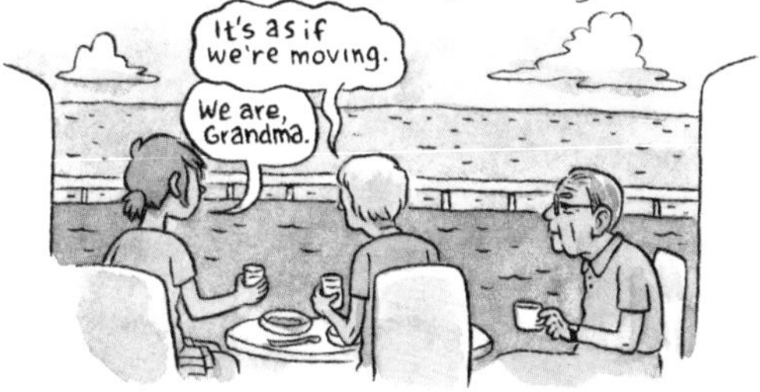
It's as if we're moving.
We are, Grandma.

My grandparents have a lot of stuff with the insignia from my grandfather's army division...

Today they look like 3rd Armored Division superheroes.

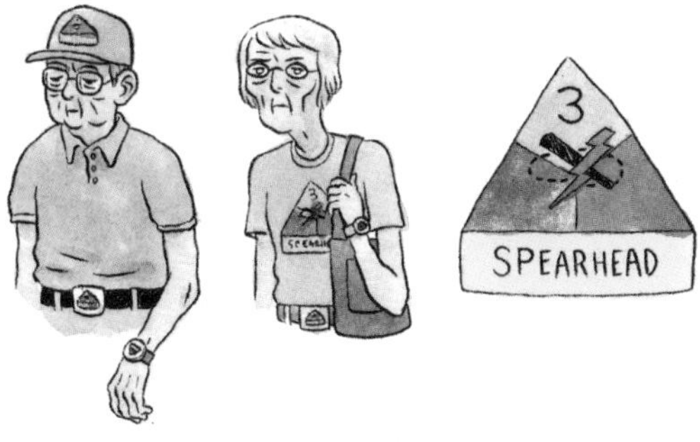
3
SPEARHEAD

...IT OCCURS TO ME:

My grands no longer read...

...And they're limited physically...

...They don't want to gamble in the casino...

They have no interest in swimming...

...And they can't sit for long periods of time.

WHAT ARE WE GONNA DO ALL WEEK!?

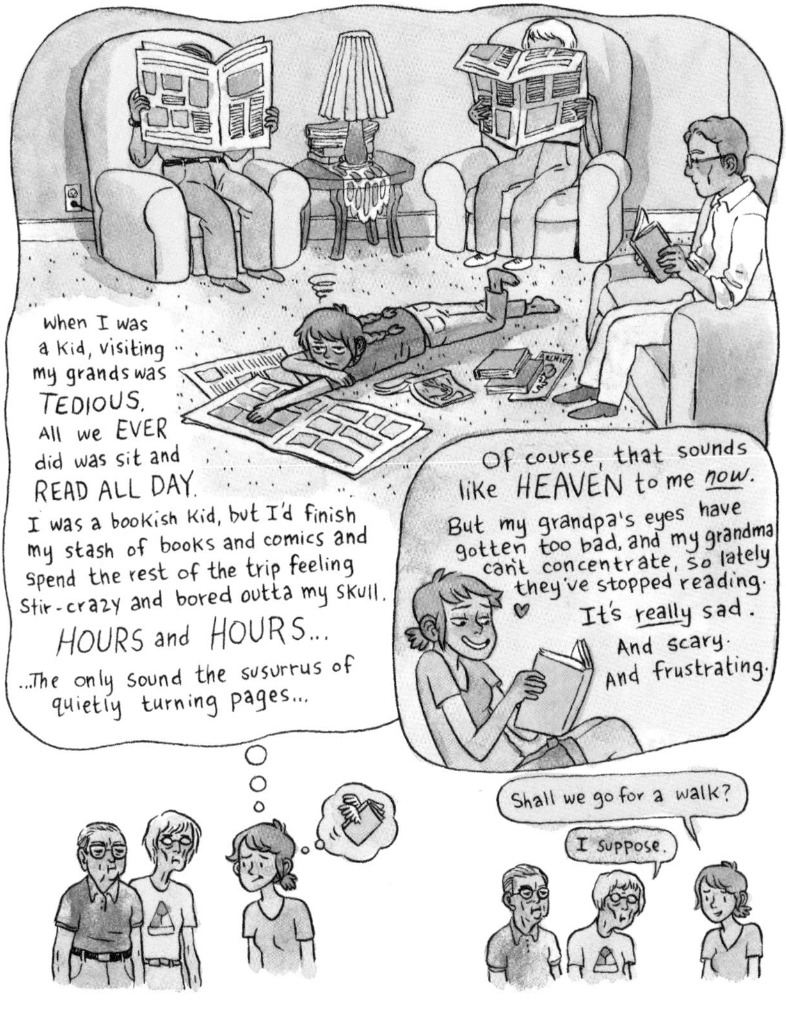

When I was a kid, visiting my grands was TEDIOUS. All we EVER did was sit and READ ALL DAY.
I was a bookish kid, but I'd finish my stash of books and comics and spend the rest of the trip feeling stir-crazy and bored outta my skull.
HOURS and HOURS...
...The only sound the susurrus of quietly turning pages...
Of course, that sounds like HEAVEN to me now.
But my grandpa's eyes have gotten too bad, and my grandma can't concentrate, so lately they've stopped reading.
It's really sad.
And scary.
And frustrating.
Shall we go for a walk?
I suppose.

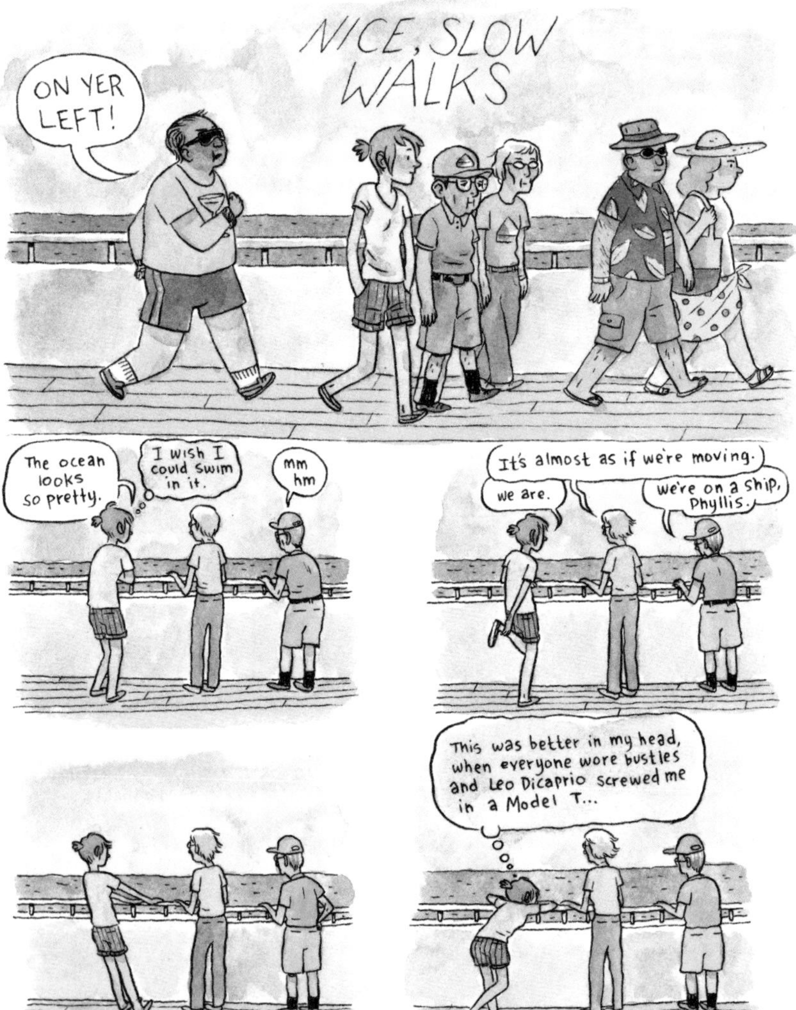
NICE, SLOW WALKS
ON YER LEFT!
The ocean looks so pretty.
I wish I could swim in it.
mm hm
It's almost as if we're moving.
we are.
we're on a ship, Phyllis.
This was better in my head, when everyone wore bustles and Leo Dicaprio screwed me in a Model T...

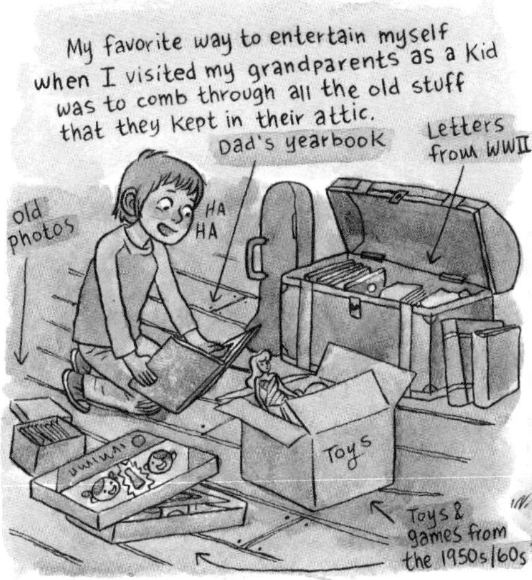
My favorite way to entertain myself when I visited my grandparents as a kid was to comb through all the old stuff that they kept in their attic.
Dad's yearbook
Letters from WWII
old photos
HA HA
Toys
Toys & games from the 1950s/60s

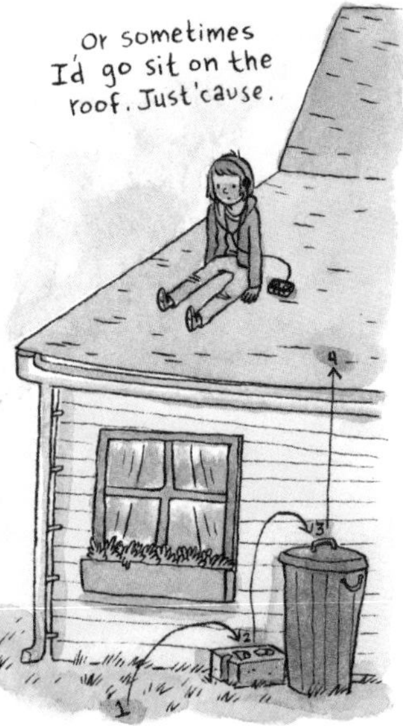
Or sometimes I'd go sit on the roof. Just 'cause.
1
2
3
4

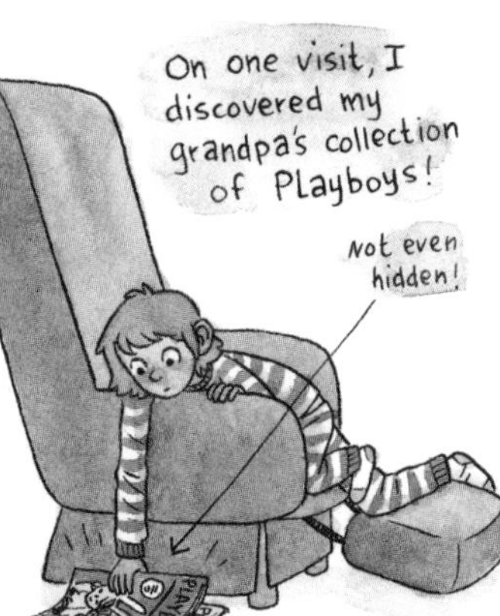
On one visit, I discovered my grandpa's collection of Playboys!
Not even hidden!
PLAYBOY

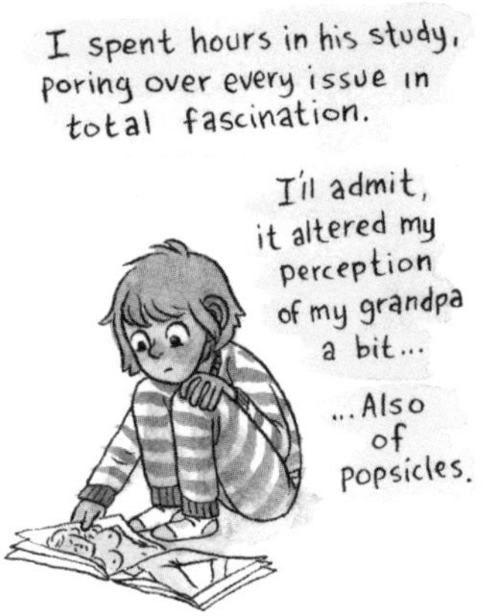
I spent hours in his study, poring over every issue in total fascination.
I'll admit, it altered my perception of my grandpa a bit...
...Also of popsicles.

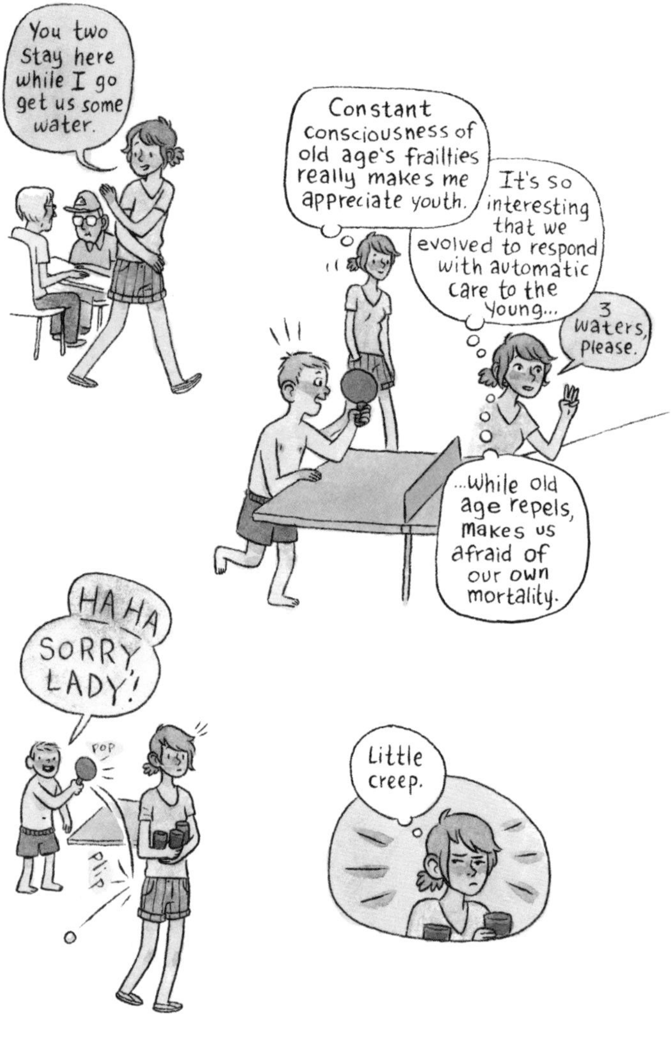
You two stay here while I go get us some water.
Constant consciousness of old age's frailties really makes me appreciate youth.
It's so interesting that we evolved to respond with automatic care to the young...
3 waters, please.
...while old age repels, makes us afraid of our own mortality.
HA HA
SORRY LADY!
POP
PLIP
Little creep.

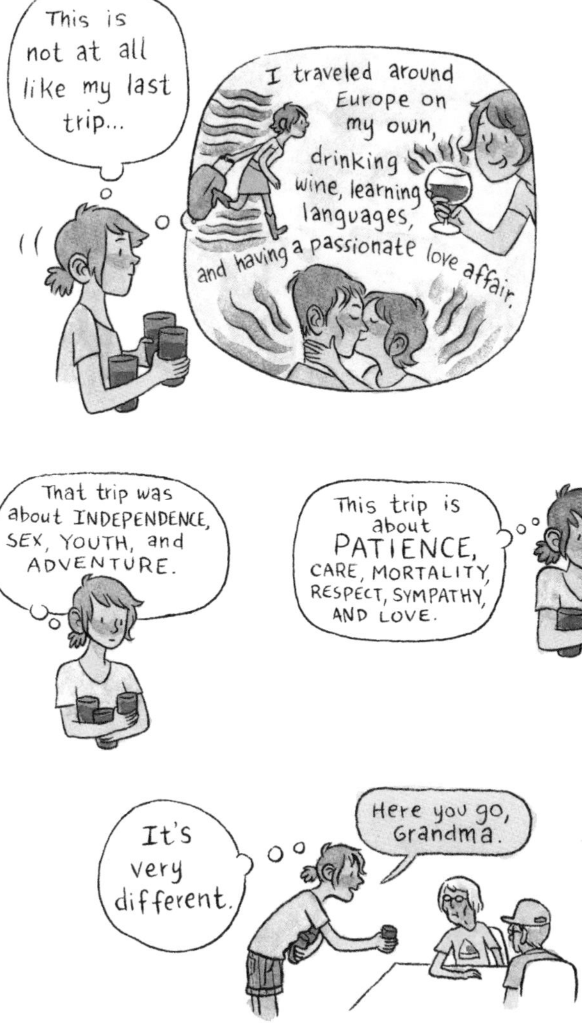
This is not at all like my last trip...
I traveled around Europe on my own, drinking wine, learning languages, and having a passionate love affair.
That trip was about INDEPENDENCE, SEX, YOUTH, and ADVENTURE.
This trip is about PATIENCE, CARE, MORTALITY, RESPECT, SYMPATHY, AND LOVE.
It's very different.
Here you go, Grandma.

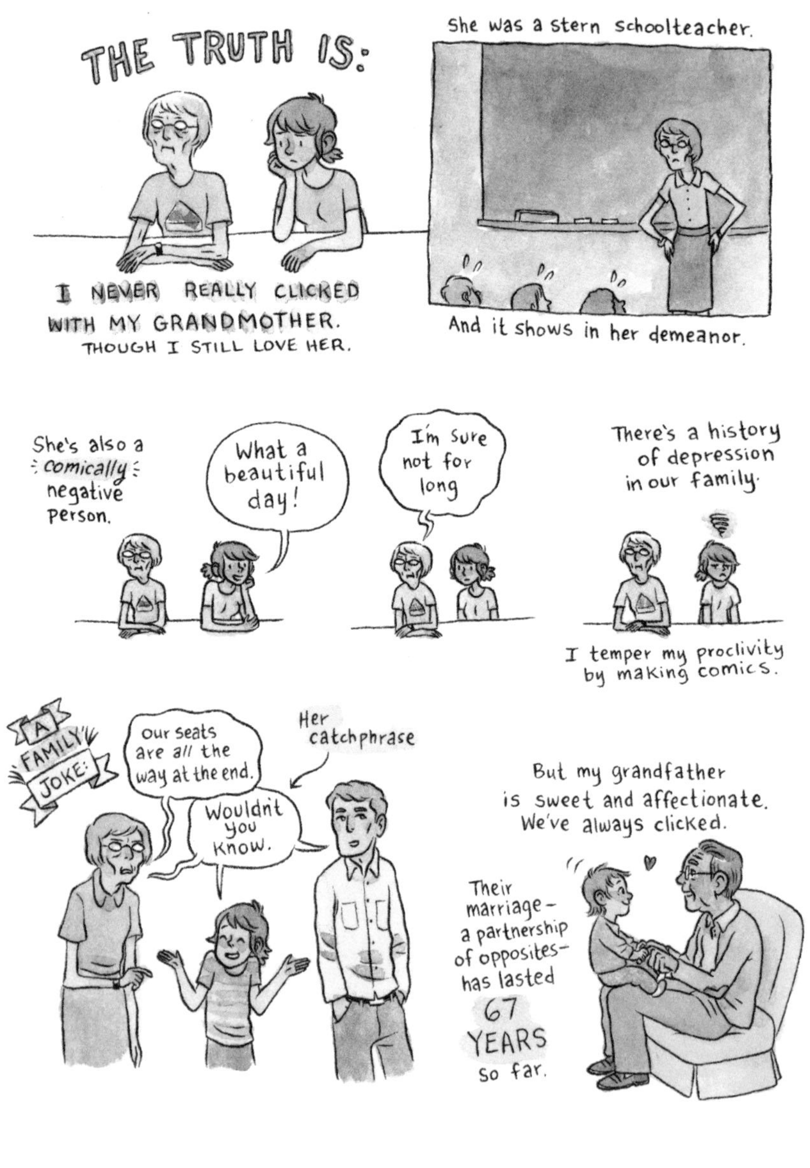
THE TRUTH IS:
I NEVER REALLY CLICKED WITH MY GRANDMOTHER.
THOUGH I STILL LOVE HER.
She was a stern schoolteacher.
And it shows in her demeanor.
She's also a comically negative person.
What a beautiful day!
I'm sure not for long
There's a history of depression in our family.
I temper my proclivity by making comics.
A FAMILY JOKE:
Our seats are all the way at the end.
Her catchphrase
Wouldn't you know.
But my grandfather is sweet and affectionate. We've always clicked.
Their marriage - a partnership of opposites - has lasted 67 YEARS so far.

We go to our tour group's little cocktail party at one of the ship's bars.

Drinking with strangers FREAKS ME OUT.

Not a big drinker

Be right back!

BRIEF PANIC ATTACK

Help!

Why am I here taking care of my grandparents by myself!?

Maybe I'll get norovirus and they'll airlift us out!

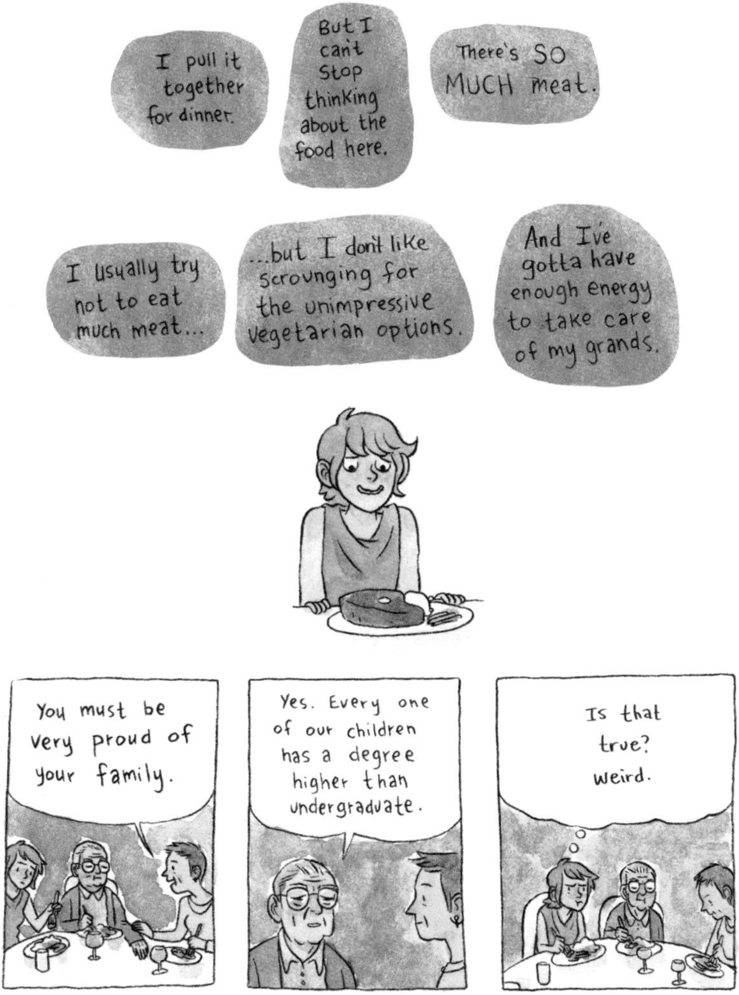
I pull it together for dinner.
But I can't stop thinking about the food here.
There's SO MUCH meat.
I usually try not to eat much meat...
...but I don't like scrounging for the unimpressive vegetarian options.
And I've gotta have enough energy to take care of my grands.
You must be very proud of your family.
Yes. Every one of our children has a degree higher than undergraduate.
Is that true? weird.

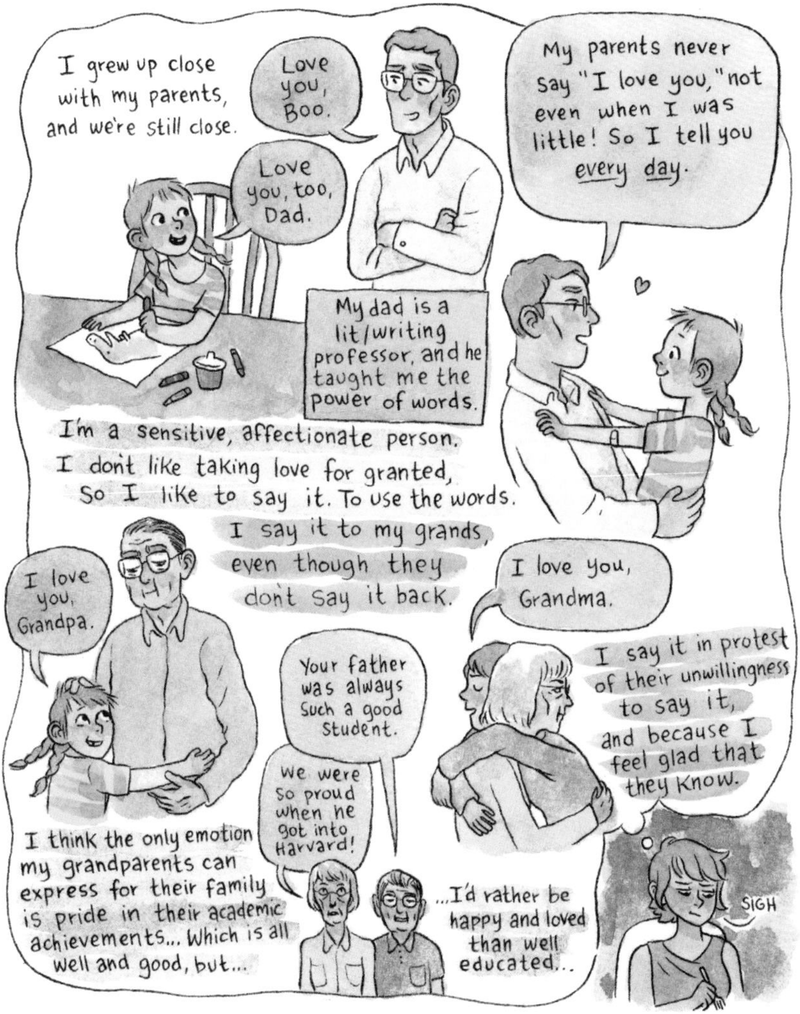

I grew up close with my parents, and we're still close.
Love you, Boo.
Love you, too, Dad.
My dad is a lit/writing professor, and he taught me the power of words.
My parents never say "I love you," not even when I was little! So I tell you every day.
I'm a sensitive, affectionate person. I don't like taking love for granted, so I like to say it. To use the words.
I say it to my grands, even though they don't say it back.
I love you, Grandpa.
I love you, Grandma.
I say it in protest of their unwillingness to say it, and because I feel glad that they know.
Your father was always such a good student.
We were so proud when he got into Harvard!
I think the only emotion my grandparents can express for their family is pride in their academic achievements... Which is all well and good, but...
...I'd rather be happy and loved than well educated...
SIGH

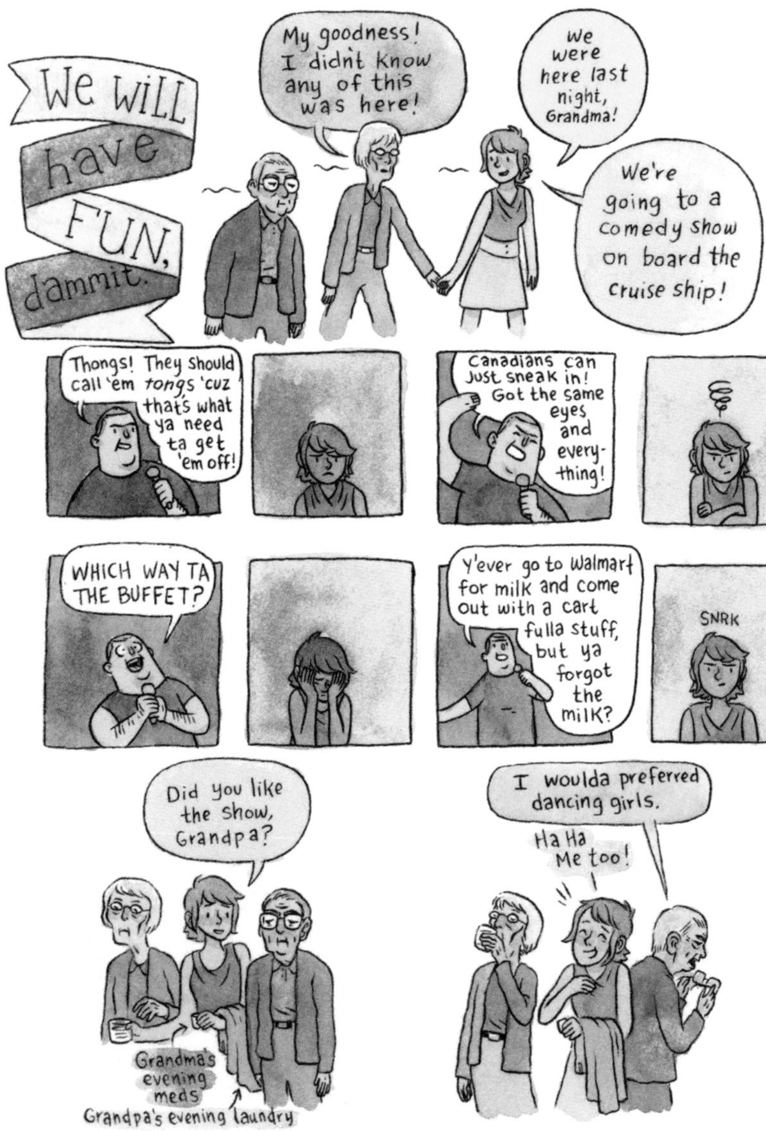
We will have FUN, dammit.
My goodness! I didn't know any of this was here!
We were here last night, Grandma!
We're going to a comedy show on board the cruise ship!
Thongs! They should call 'em *tongs* 'cuz that's what ya need ta get 'em off!
Canadians can just sneak in! Got the same eyes and every-thing!
WHICH WAY TA THE BUFFET?
Y'ever go to Walmart for milk and come out with a cart fulla stuff, but ya forgot the milk?
SNRK
Did you like the show, Grandpa?
Grandma's evening meds
Grandpa's evening laundry
I woulda preferred dancing girls.
Ha Ha Me too!

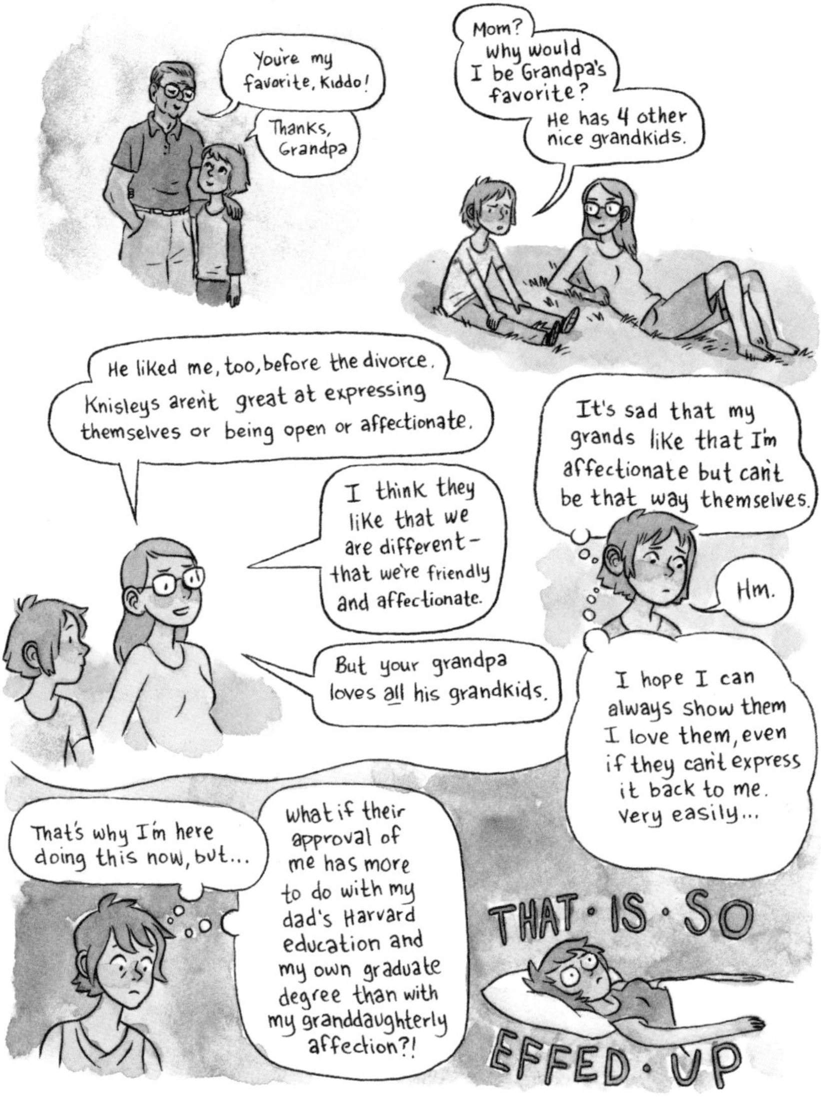

You're my favorite, Kiddo!
Thanks, Grandpa
Mom? Why would I be Grandpa's favorite?
He has 4 other nice grandkids.
He liked me, too, before the divorce. Knisleys aren't great at expressing themselves or being open or affectionate.
I think they like that we are different - that we're friendly and affectionate.
But your grandpa loves all his grandkids.
It's sad that my grands like that I'm affectionate but can't be that way themselves.
Hm.
I hope I can always show them I love them, even if they can't express it back to me very easily...
That's why I'm here doing this now, but...
What if their approval of me has more to do with my dad's Harvard education and my own graduate degree than with my granddaughterly affection?!
THAT · IS · SO EFFED · UP

Insomnia Funtime

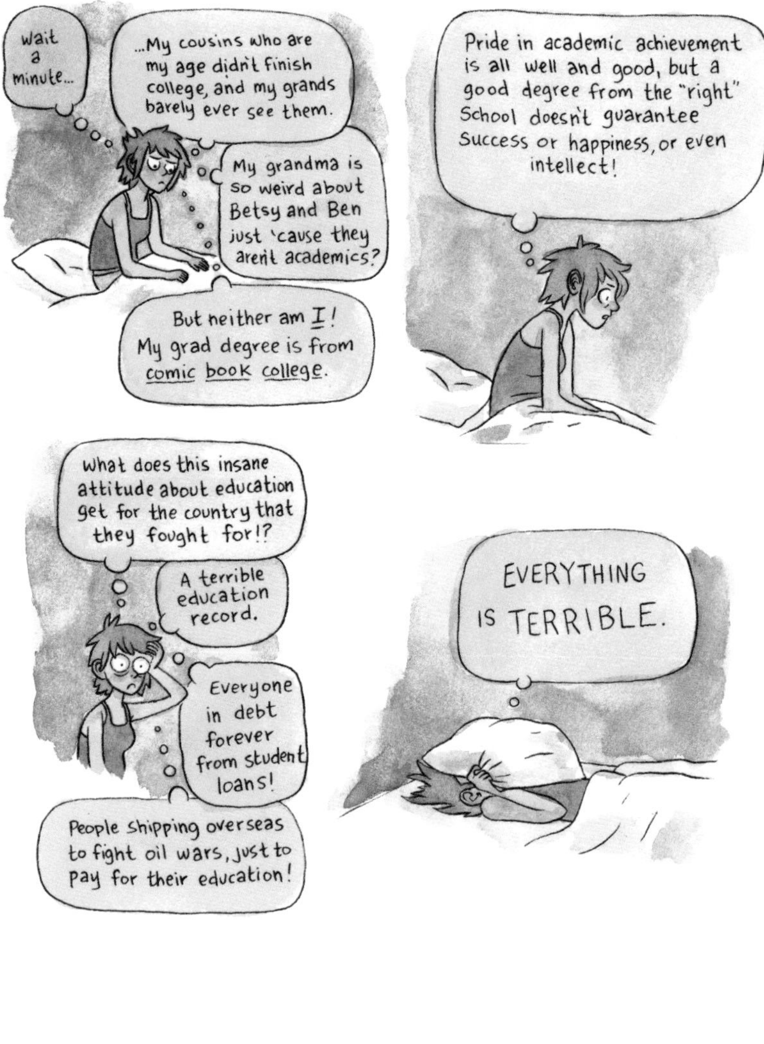

Wait a minute...
...My cousins who are my age didn't finish college, and my grands barely ever see them.
My grandma is so weird about Betsy and Ben just 'cause they aren't academics?
But neither am I! My grad degree is from comic book college.
Pride in academic achievement is all well and good, but a good degree from the "right" School doesn't guarantee Success or happiness, or even intellect!
What does this insane attitude about education get for the country that they fought for!?
A terrible education record.
Everyone in debt forever from student loans!
People shipping overseas to fight oil wars, just to pay for their education!
EVERYTHING IS TERRIBLE.

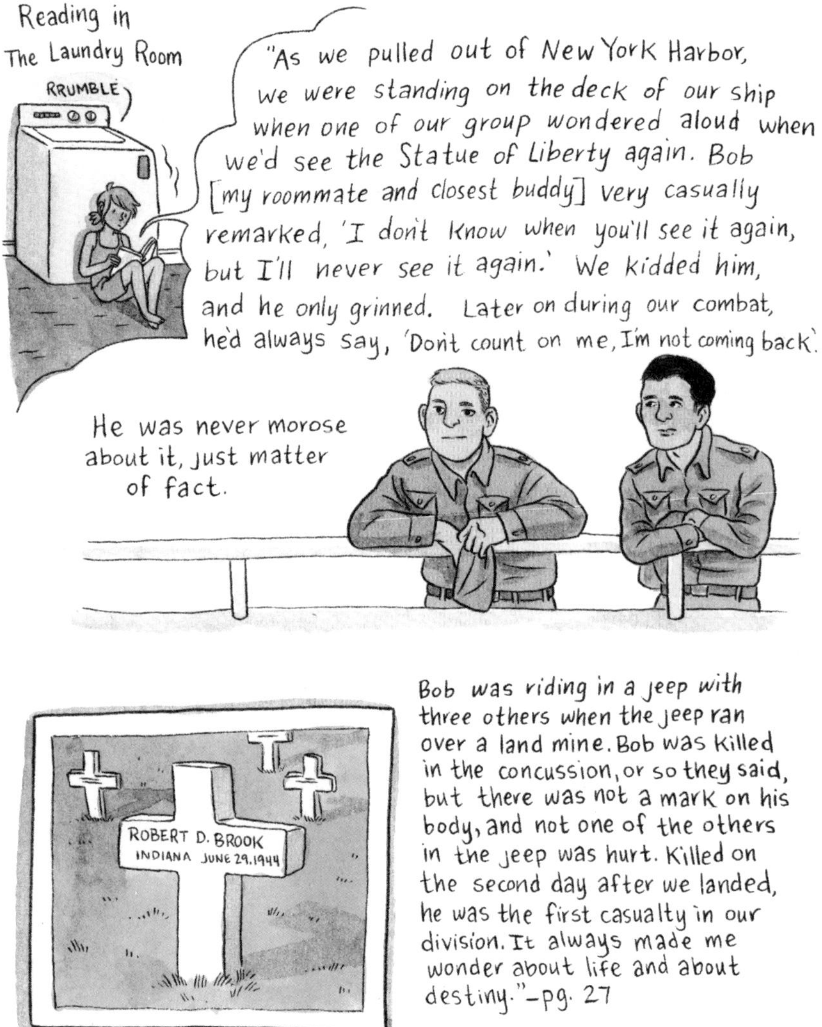
Reading in The Laundry Room
RRUMBLE
"As we pulled out of New York Harbor, we were standing on the deck of our ship when one of our group wondered aloud when we'd see the Statue of Liberty again. Bob [my roommate and closest buddy] very casually remarked, 'I don't know when you'll see it again, but I'll never see it again.' We kidded him, and he only grinned. Later on during our combat, he'd always say, 'Don't count on me, I'm not coming back.'
He was never morose about it, just matter of fact.
ROBERT D. BROOK
INDIANA JUNE 29, 1944
Bob was riding in a jeep with three others when the jeep ran over a land mine. Bob was killed in the concussion, or so they said, but there was not a mark on his body, and not one of the others in the jeep was hurt. Killed on the second day after we landed, he was the first casualty in our division. It always made me wonder about life and about destiny."–pg. 27

Day 5

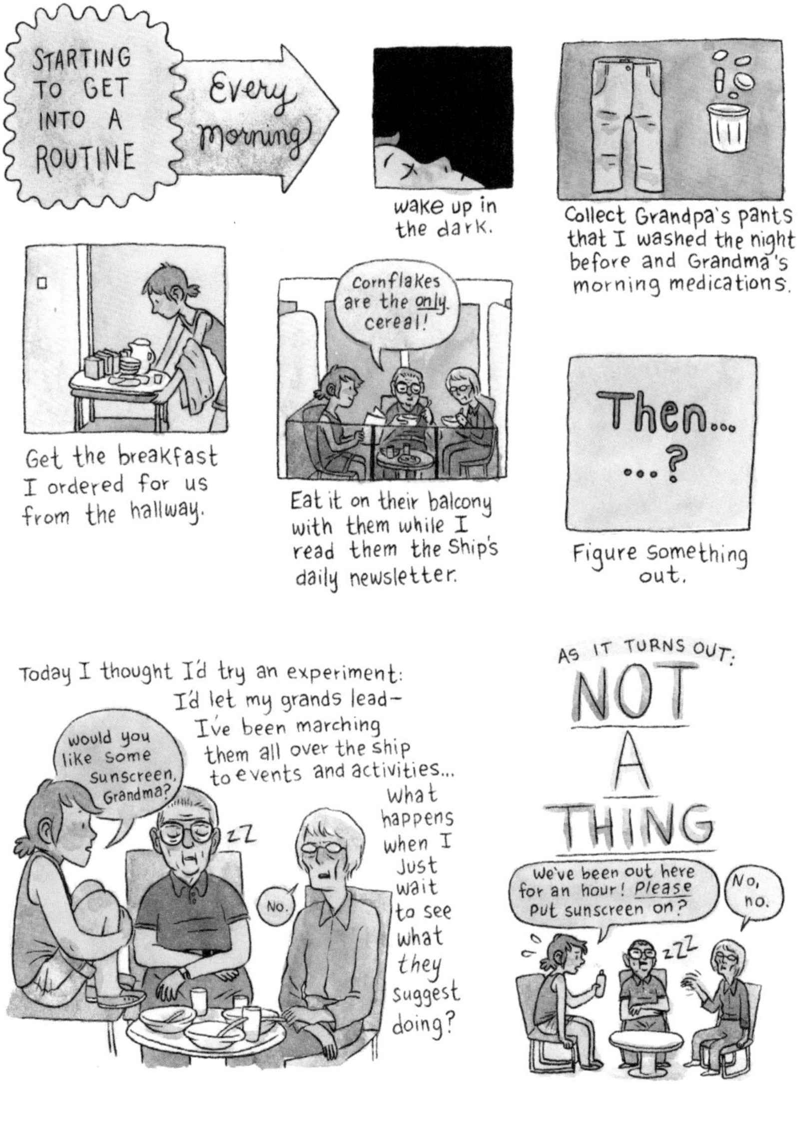
STARTING TO GET INTO A ROUTINE
Every morning
wake up in the dark.
Collect Grandpa's pants that I washed the night before and Grandma's morning medications.
Get the breakfast I ordered for us from the hallway.
Cornflakes are the only cereal!
Eat it on their balcony with them while I read them the ship's daily newsletter.
Then...
...?
Figure something out.
Today I thought I'd try an experiment:
I'd let my grands lead–
I've been marching them all over the ship to events and activities...
What happens when I just wait to see what they suggest doing?
would you like some sunscreen, Grandma?
zZ
No.
AS IT TURNS OUT:
NOT A THING
We've been out here for an hour! Please put sunscreen on?
zZZ
No, no.

Some of the disturbing things I discovered while unpacking my grands' things:

About *ten* packaged toothbrushes

Six or seven toothpastes

four or five combs

BUT NOW

Let's go to the ship shop to see if we can find some sunglasses for Grandpa.

Anything else ya wanna get?

I need toothpicks... I forgot my toothbrush.

I'd like to pick up a pocket comb.

They don't have toothpicks or clippie sunglasses, but we bought a new comb and toothbrush.

It was easier than forcing them to confront their packing situation.

I Am Finding New Ways Every Day To Get Yelled At.

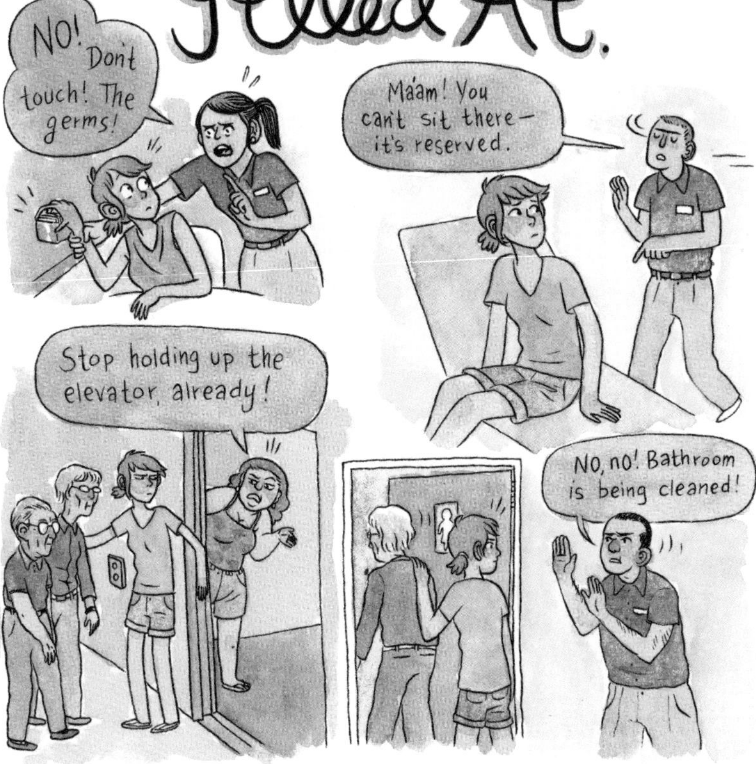

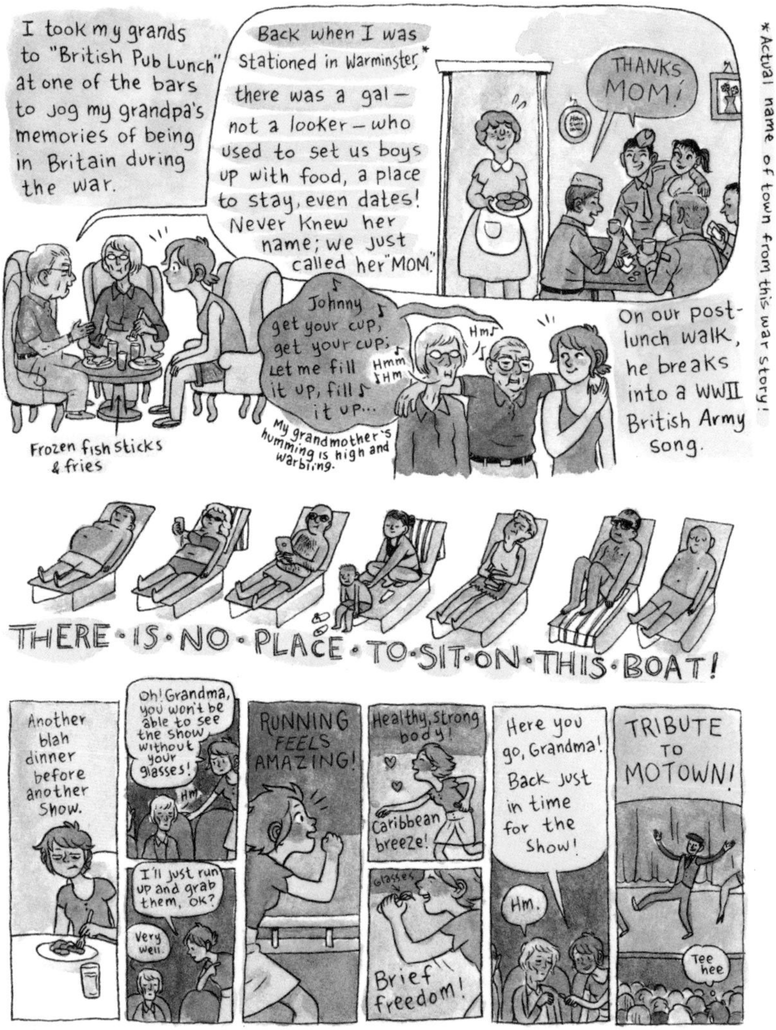
I took my grands to "British Pub Lunch" at one of the bars to jog my grandpa's memories of being in Britain during the war.
Back when I was stationed in Warminster,* there was a gal — not a looker — who used to set us boys up with food, a place to stay, even dates! Never knew her name; we just called her "MOM."
THANKS MOM!
*Actual name of town from this war story!
Frozen fish sticks & fries
Johnny get your cup, get your cup; let me fill it up, fill it up...
Hmm Hm
Hm
My grandmother's humming is high and warbling.
On our post-lunch walk, he breaks into a WWII British Army song.
THERE · IS · NO · PLACE · TO · SIT · ON · THIS · BOAT!
Another blah dinner before another show.
Oh! Grandma, you won't be able to see the show without your glasses!
Hm
I'll just run up and grab them, OK?
Very well.
RUNNING FEELS AMAZING!
Healthy, strong body!
Caribbean breeze!
Glasses
Brief freedom!
Here you go, Grandma! Back just in time for the show!
Hm.
TRIBUTE TO MOTOWN!
Tee hee

I can't help getting a bit freaked out when sitting across from

DAVE.

He is very intense.
And his fingernails...

I really wish
he would direct
his stare elsewhere...

I know it's selfish —
that it's mostly a manifestation of
my frustration and worry over my
grandparents' declining physical abilities...

...but I really miss my regular walking pace.
We go to the show.

Costumes by the Mattel Barbie corporation!

Did you like the show, Grandma?

Are you a person I Know?

...Let's get to bed.

After evening meds & bedtime reassurances
BACK · IN · MY · OWN · ROOM
SIGH
This call will be $4.50 per minute.
Calling DAD
Hi, Boo!
How's it going?
Not great.
This has been pretty hard on Grandma & Grandpa.
The air travel especially...
Grandma's... pretty out of it.
Yeah.
If I get to that point, just kill me.
Dad, that's not helpful.
We need to improve this for them – get them a direct flight home, maybe?
I'll see about it.
Hang in there, Boo.
Thanks, Dad.
Love you.
Love you.
$45 call!
CLICK

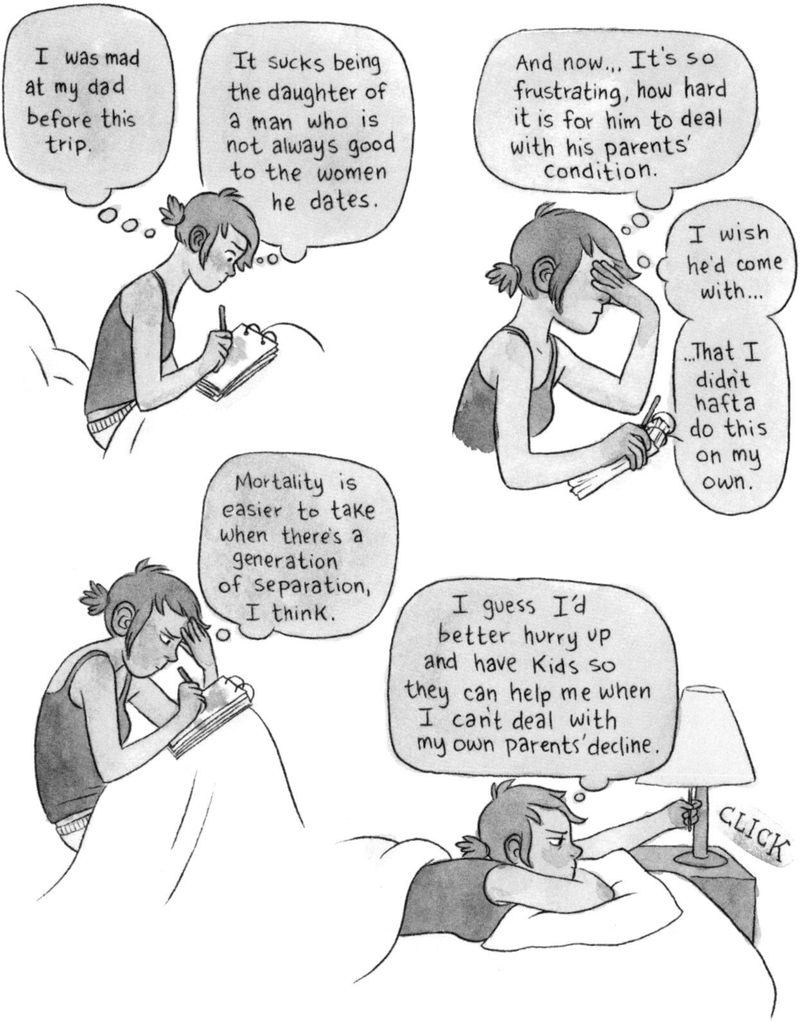
I was mad at my dad before this trip.
It sucks being the daughter of a man who is not always good to the women he dates.
And now... It's so frustrating, how hard it is for him to deal with his parents' condition.
I wish he'd come with...
...That I didn't hafta do this on my own.
Mortality is easier to take when there's a generation of separation, I think.
I guess I'd better hurry up and have Kids so they can help me when I can't deal with my own parents' decline.
CLICK

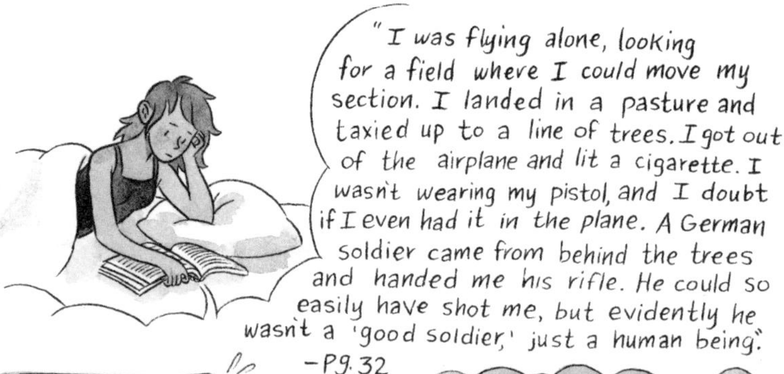
"I was flying alone, looking for a field where I could move my section. I landed in a pasture and taxied up to a line of trees. I got out of the airplane and lit a cigarette. I wasn't wearing my pistol, and I doubt if I even had it in the plane. A German soldier came from behind the trees and handed me his rifle. He could so easily have shot me, but evidently he wasn't a 'good soldier,' just a human being."
-Pg. 32

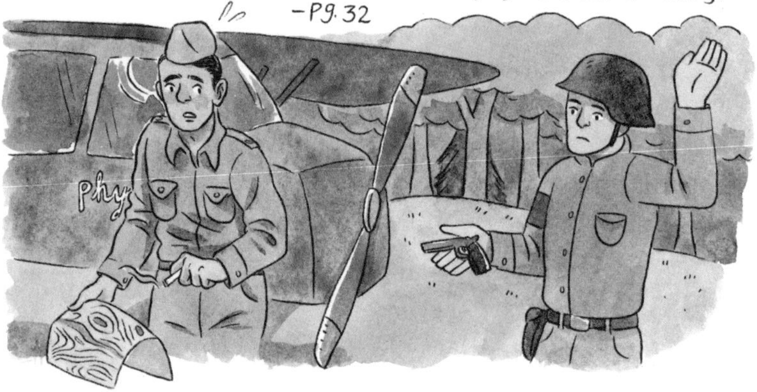

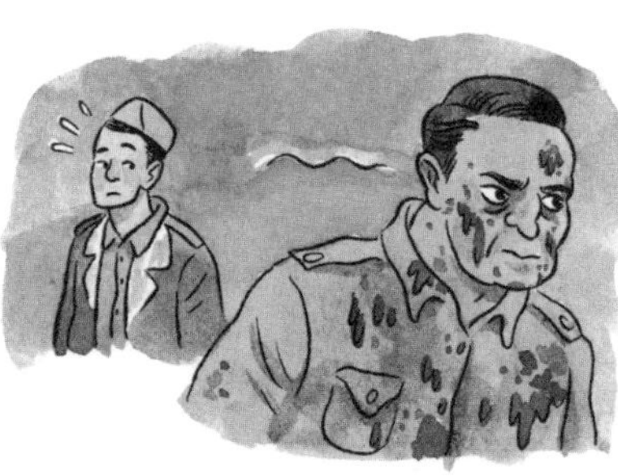

"I had a mechanic's helper, a private named Henry Pickering. Ugly, and mean as sin, especially when he was drunk, and he often was. I never trusted him. One night he came staggering in, covered with blood and mud. The next morning, we found a poor butchered dead Frenchman near our camp. I'm almost positive that Pickering killed him, but he denied it, and I had no proof."

-Pg. 33

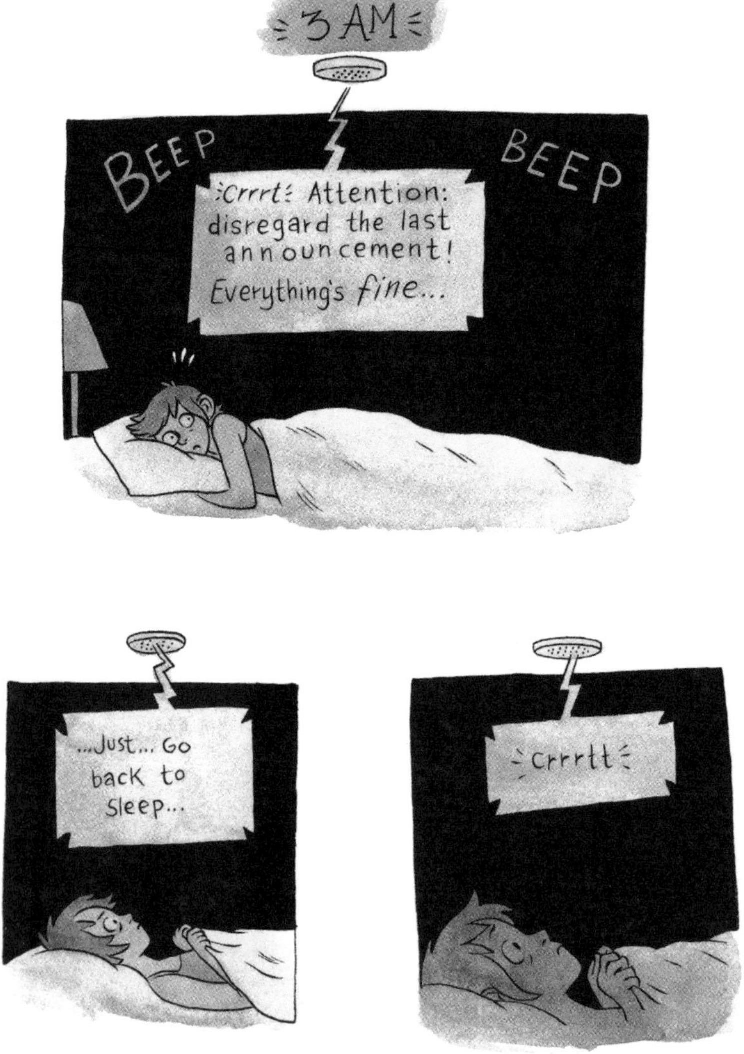
3 AM
BEEP
BEEP
Crrrt Attention: disregard the last announcement! Everything's fine...
...Just... Go back to sleep...
Crrrtt

Day 6

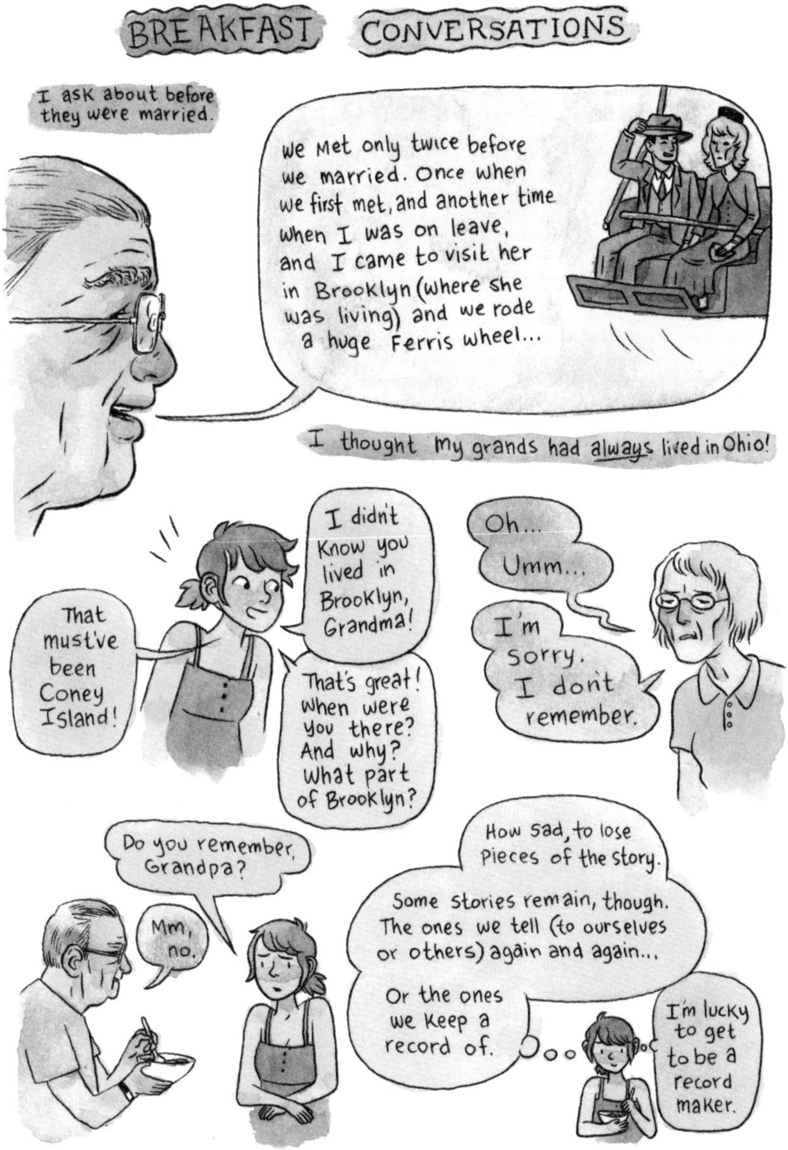
BREAKFAST CONVERSATIONS
I ask about before they were married.
We met only twice before we married. Once when we first met, and another time when I was on leave, and I came to visit her in Brooklyn (where she was living) and we rode a huge Ferris wheel...
I thought my grands had always lived in Ohio!
I didn't know you lived in Brooklyn, Grandma!
That must've been Coney Island!
That's great! When were you there? And why? What part of Brooklyn?
Oh...
Umm...
I'm sorry. I don't remember.
Do you remember, Grandpa?
Mm, no.
How sad, to lose pieces of the story.
Some stories remain, though. The ones we tell (to ourselves or others) again and again...
Or the ones we keep a record of.
I'm lucky to get to be a record maker.

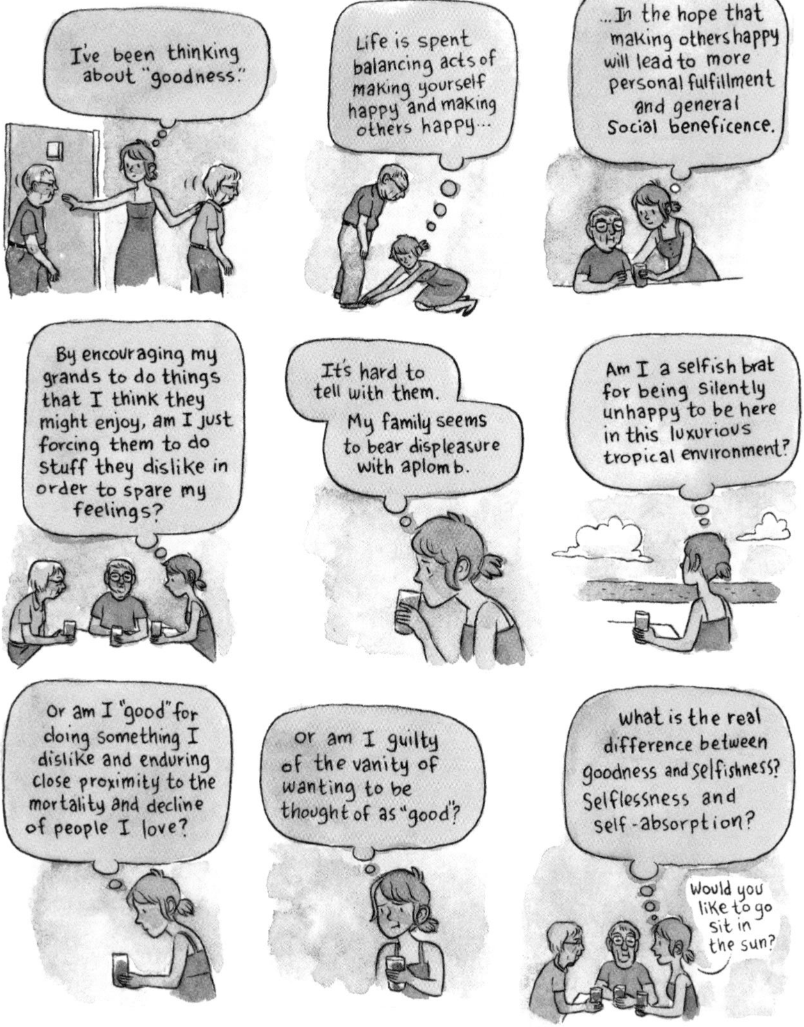
I've been thinking about "goodness."
Life is spent balancing acts of making yourself happy and making others happy...
...In the hope that making others happy will lead to more personal fulfillment and general Social beneficence.
By encouraging my grands to do things that I think they might enjoy, am I just forcing them to do stuff they dislike in order to spare my feelings?
It's hard to tell with them.
My family seems to bear displeasure with aplomb.
Am I a selfish brat for being silently unhappy to be here in this luxurious tropical environment?
Or am I "good" for doing something I dislike and enduring close proximity to the mortality and decline of people I love?
Or am I guilty of the vanity of wanting to be thought of as "good"?
What is the real difference between goodness and selfishness? Selflessness and self-absorption?
Would you like to go sit in the sun?

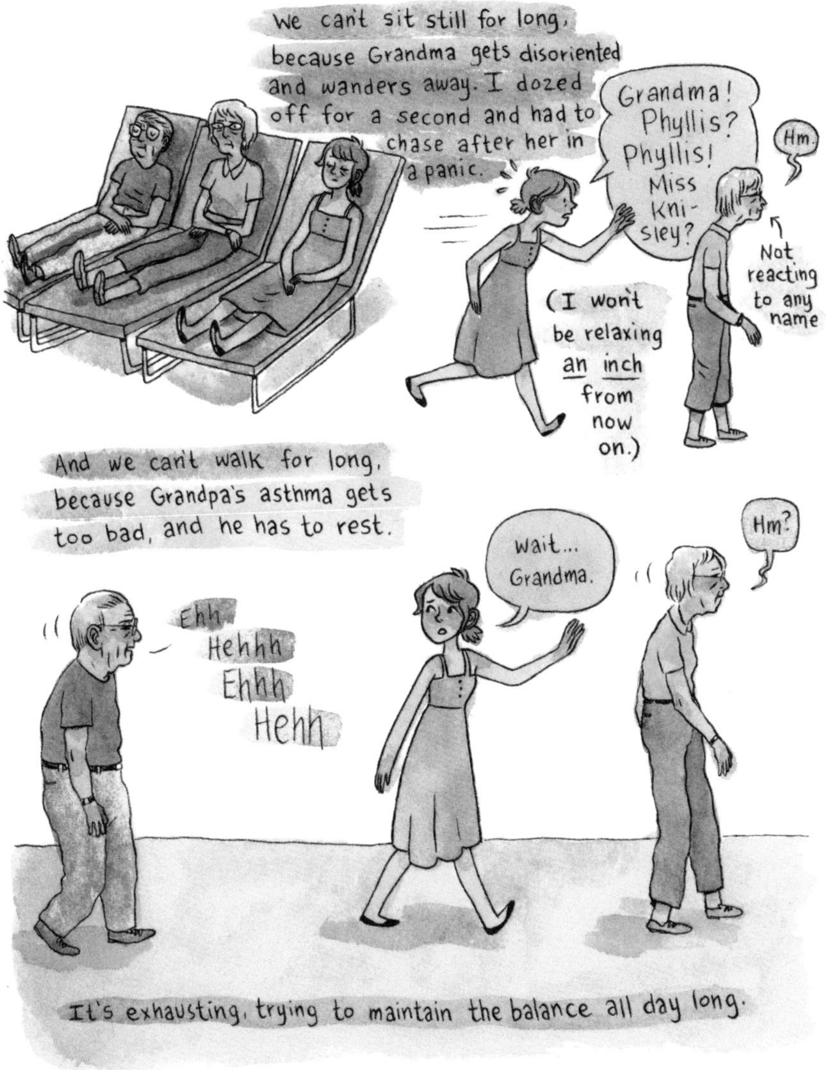
We can't sit still for long, because Grandma gets disoriented and wanders away. I dozed off for a second and had to chase after her in a panic.
Grandma! Phyllis? Phyllis! Miss Kni-sley?
Hm.
Not reacting to any name
(I won't be relaxing an inch from now on.)
And we can't walk for long, because Grandpa's asthma gets too bad, and he has to rest.
Ehh Hehhh Ehhh Hehh
Wait... Grandma.
Hm?
It's exhausting, trying to maintain the balance all day long.

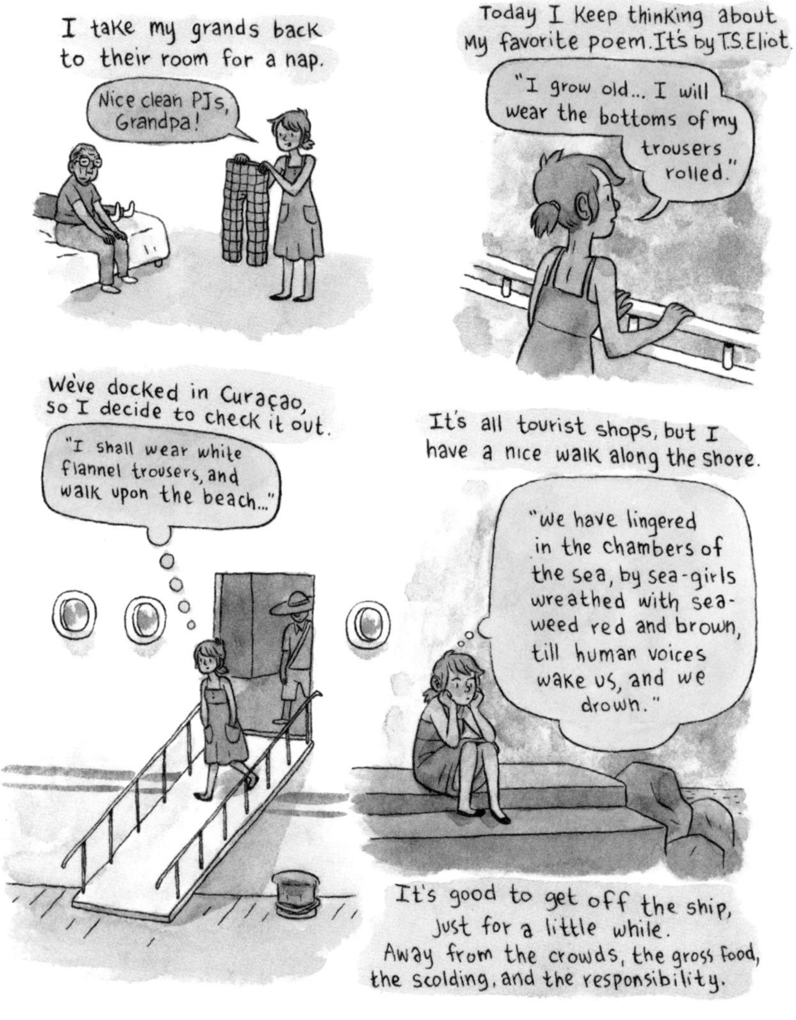
I take my grands back to their room for a nap.
Nice clean PJs, Grandpa!
Today I keep thinking about my favorite poem. It's by T.S. Eliot.
"I grow old... I will wear the bottoms of my trousers rolled."
We've docked in Curaçao, so I decide to check it out.
"I shall wear white flannel trousers, and walk upon the beach..."
It's all tourist shops, but I have a nice walk along the shore.
"we have lingered in the chambers of the sea, by sea-girls wreathed with sea-weed red and brown, till human voices wake us, and we drown."
It's good to get off the ship, just for a little while.
Away from the crowds, the gross food, the scolding, and the responsibility.

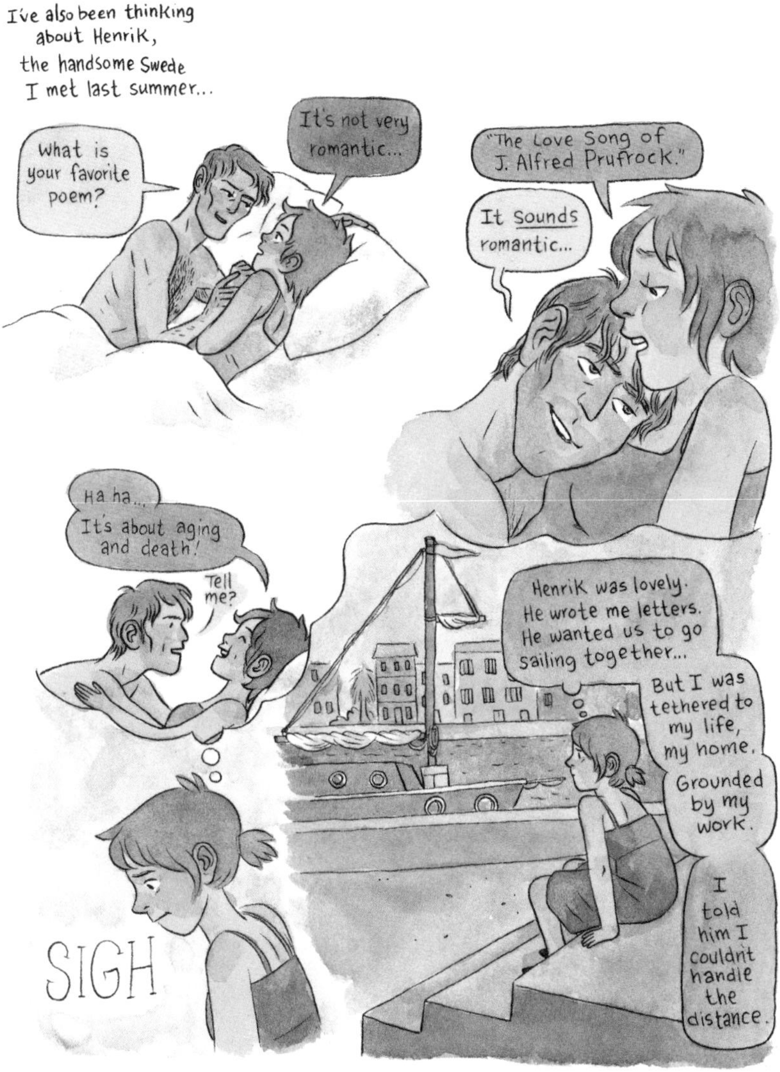
I've also been thinking about Henrik, the handsome Swede I met last summer...
What is your favorite poem?
It's not very romantic...
"The Love Song of J. Alfred Prufrock."
It sounds romantic...
Ha ha...
It's about aging and death!
Tell me?
Henrik was lovely. He wrote me letters. He wanted us to go sailing together...
But I was tethered to my life, my home.
Grounded by my work.
I told him I couldn't handle the distance.
SIGH

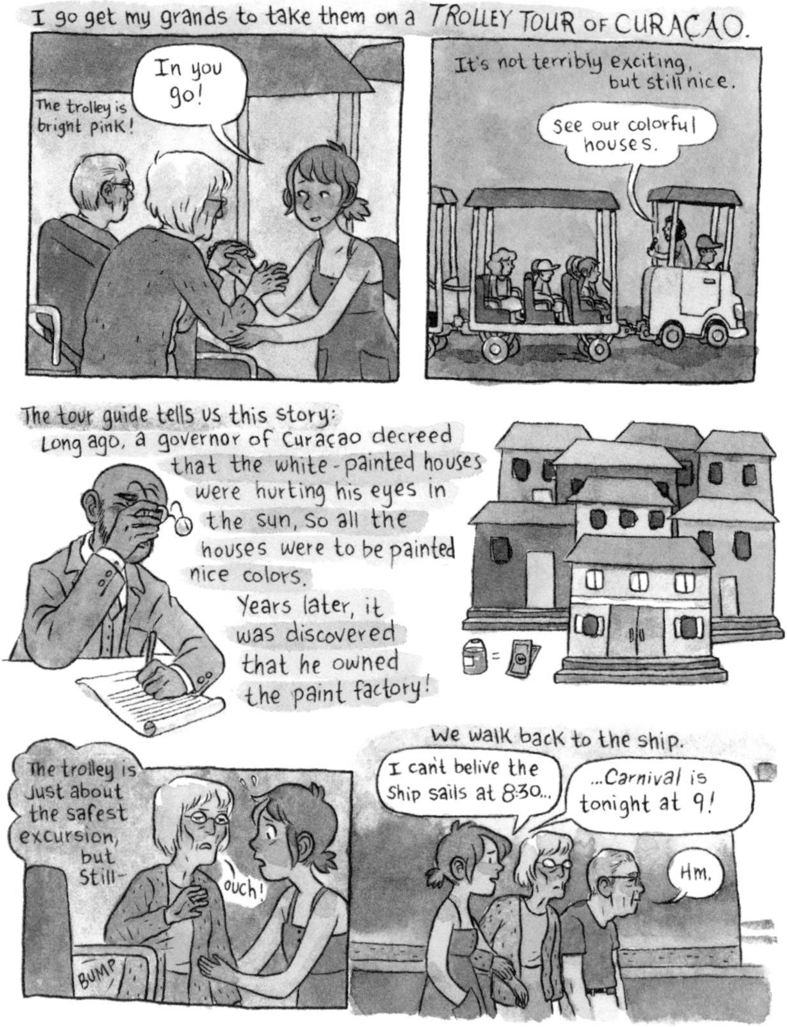
I go get my grands to take them on a TROLLEY TOUR OF CURAÇAO.
The trolley is bright pink!
In you go!
It's not terribly exciting, but still nice.
See our colorful houses.
The tour guide tells us this story:
Long ago, a governor of Curaçao decreed that the white-painted houses were hurting his eyes in the sun, so all the houses were to be painted nice colors.
Years later, it was discovered that he owned the paint factory!
The trolley is just about the safest excursion, but still-
ouch!
BUMP
We walk back to the ship.
I can't belive the ship sails at 8:30...
...Carnival is tonight at 9!
Hm.

The bump on my grandma's arm from the trolley blooms into a huge bruise.

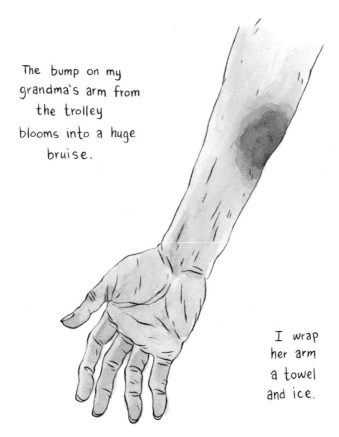

I wrap her arm a towel and ice.

I have some dinner delivered to my grands' room.
We watch "An Affair to Remember" on the TV while we eat.

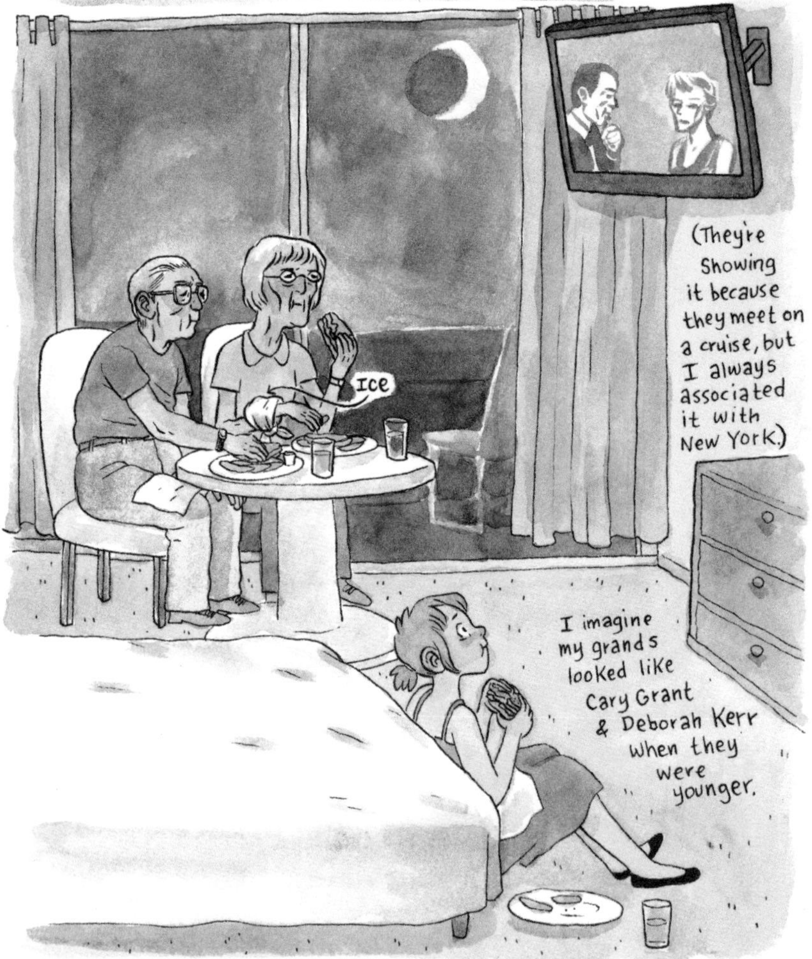
(They're showing it because they meet on a cruise, but I always associated it with New York.)
ICE
I imagine my grands looked like Cary Grant & Deborah Kerr when they were younger.

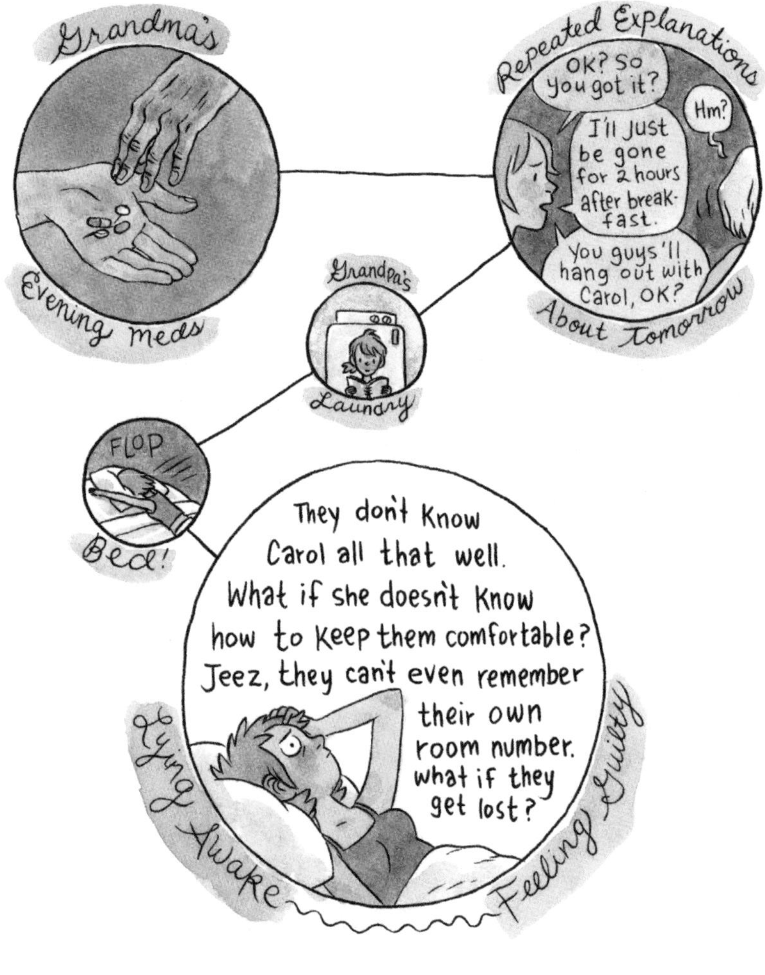
Grandma's
Evening meds
Repeated Explanations
OK? So you got it?
I'll just be gone for 2 hours after break-fast.
Hm?
You guys'll hang out with Carol, OK?
About Tomorrow
Grandpa's
Laundry
FLOP
Bed!
They don't know Carol all that well. What if she doesn't know how to keep them comfortable? Jeez, they can't even remember their own room number. what if they get lost?
Lying Awake
Feeling Guilty

"[While my battalion was billeting on a German family farm,] they did everything to make us feel welcome. They shared their food with us, we shared our rations with them, eating together around the huge kitchen table. [One time, while helping on the farm during a calf birth,] Some of us helped as 'Papa' and the girls tried to aid the process by reaching out and pulling the calf out of the cow's womb. It was a bit more than Vic, strictly a city boy, could Stomach, and he ran outside and vomited. The subject had not been covered in artillery school."

—pg. 41

"A day or two after Christmas, I was riding in our half-track vehicle on the way to batallion headquarters when the front wheel ran over the feet of a frozen dead soldier covered with snow. It caused the corpse to flip up out of the snow, right by the half-track."

—pg. 45

Day 7

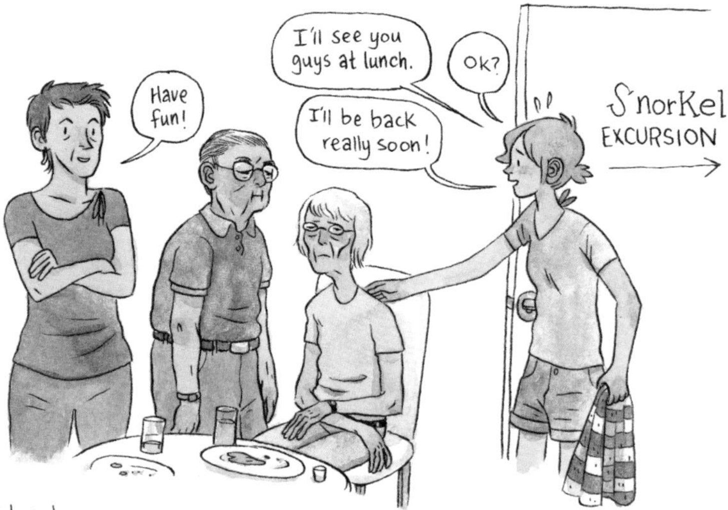
Have fun!
I'll see you guys at lunch.
Ok?
I'll be back really soon!
SnorKel EXCURSION

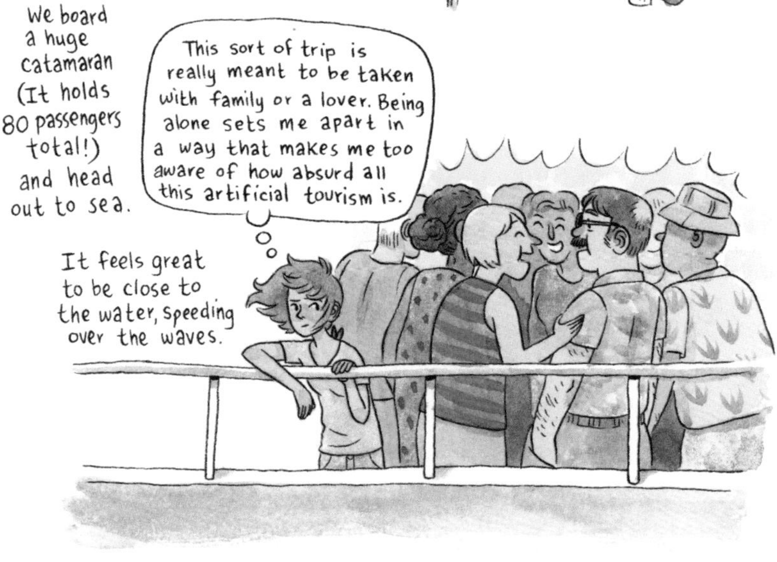
We board a huge catamaran (It holds 80 passengers total!) and head out to sea.
This sort of trip is really meant to be taken with family or a lover. Being alone sets me apart in a way that makes me too aware of how absurd all this artificial tourism is.
It feels great to be close to the water, speeding over the waves.

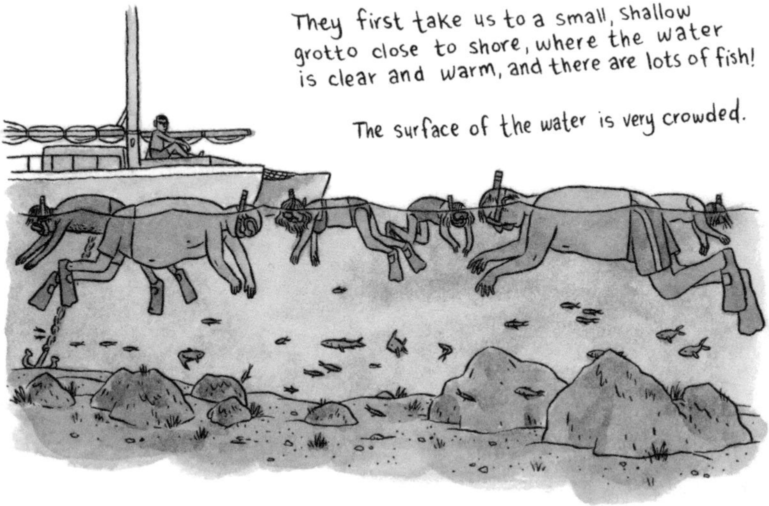
They first take us to a small, shallow grotto close to shore, where the water is clear and warm, and there are lots of fish!
The surface of the water is very crowded.

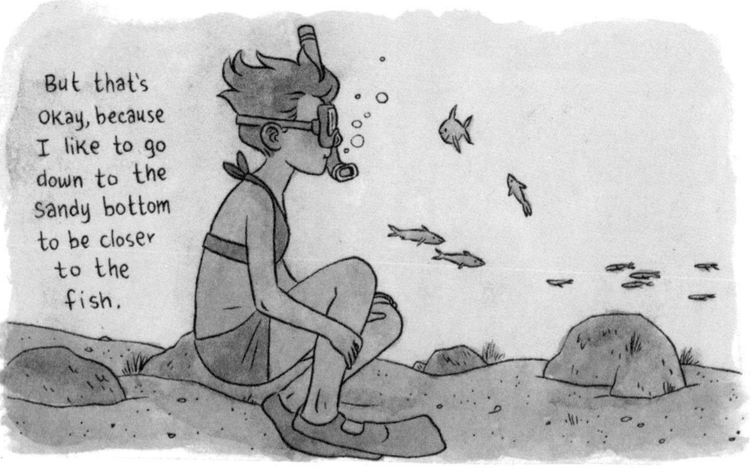
But that's okay, because I like to go down to the sandy bottom to be closer to the fish.

The boat takes us on to our 2nd (& final) diving location.

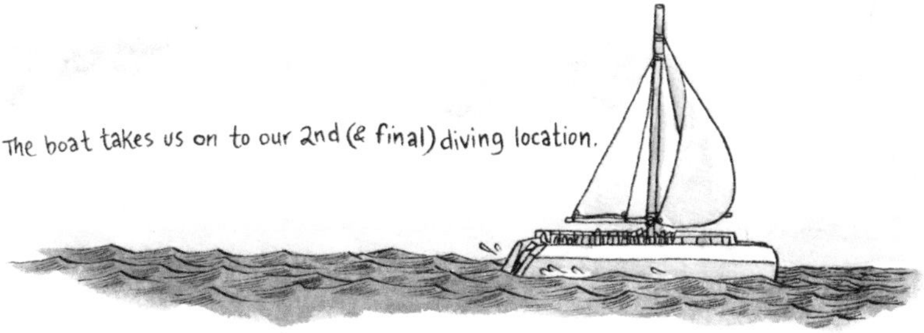

It's the site of a sunken German freighter ship: the Antilla. In the brochure, it appeared to be sunk only partially, into clear, shallow water, but that is not the case when we arrive.

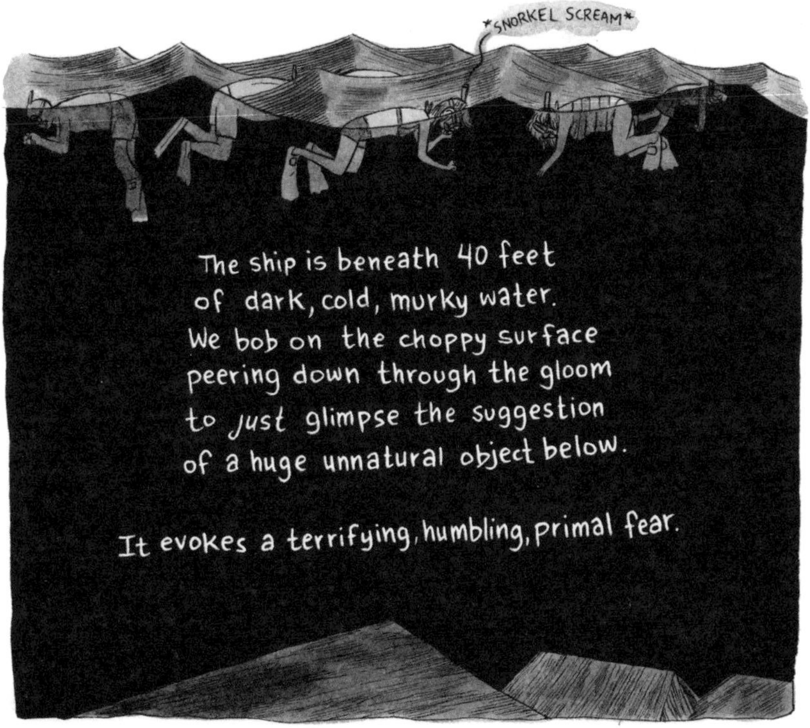
SNORKEL SCREAM
The ship is beneath 40 feet of dark, cold, murky water. We bob on the choppy surface peering down through the gloom to *just* glimpse the suggestion of a huge unnatural object below.
It evokes a terrifying, humbling, primal fear.

On the way back to the big ship, the other people on the tour drink red cocktails, singing and getting loud and unruly while I stay quiet. Even if my solitude didn't already set me apart from these loud families and boisterous couples, I'd still be silent and pensive.

That huge, dead ship filled me with something... fathomless, low, and malignant...

I try to switch my focus back from "Snorkel mode" to "caring for my grands mode".

Sailboat Hair

On my way to meet my grands and Carol for lunch at the cafeteria, I think about a piece of art by Damien Hirst that I saw when I was 16. It's called "The Physical Impossibility of Death in the Mind of Someone Living."

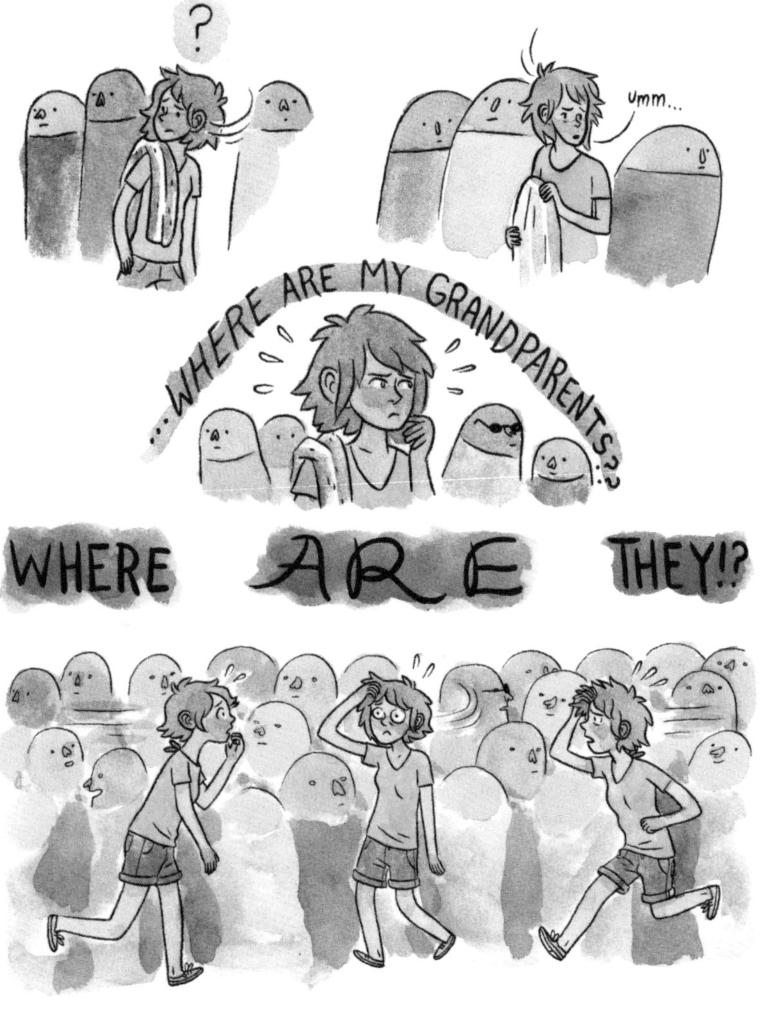
?
umm...
...WHERE ARE MY GRANDPARENTS??
WHERE ARE THEY!?

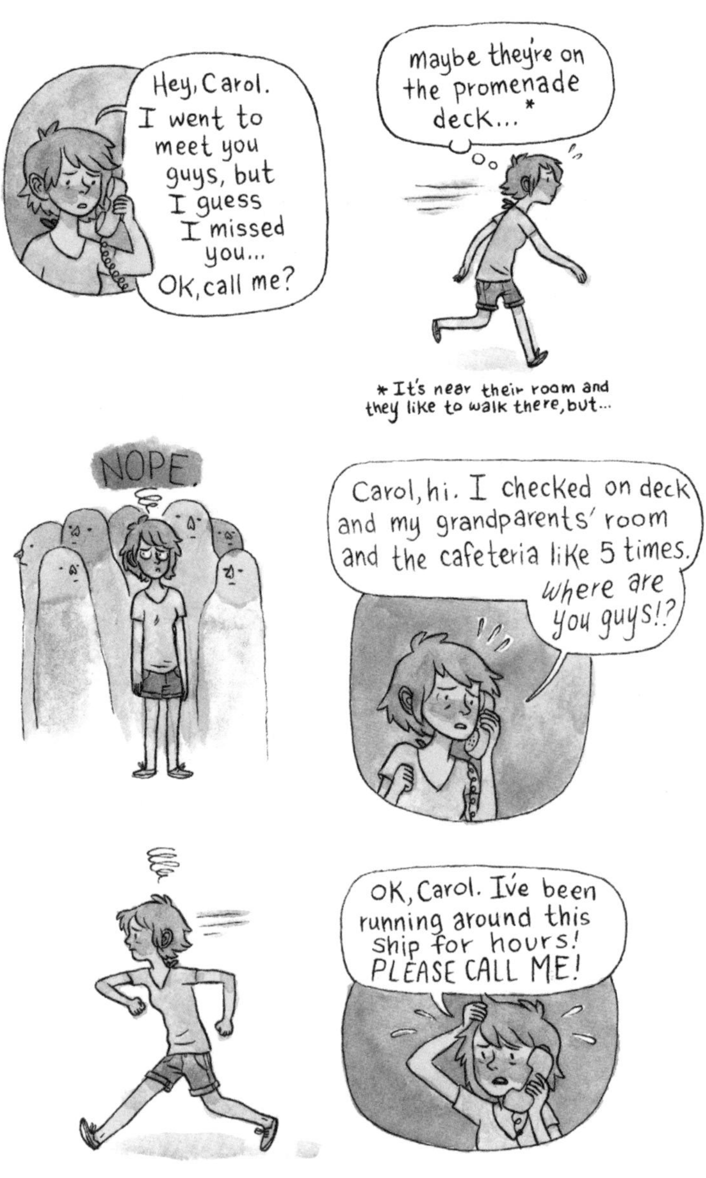
Hey, Carol. I went to meet you guys, but I guess I missed you... OK, call me?
maybe they're on the promenade deck...*
* It's near their room and they like to walk there, but...
NOPE.
Carol, hi. I checked on deck and my grandparents' room and the cafeteria like 5 times. Where are you guys!?
OK, Carol. I've been running around this ship for hours! PLEASE CALL ME!

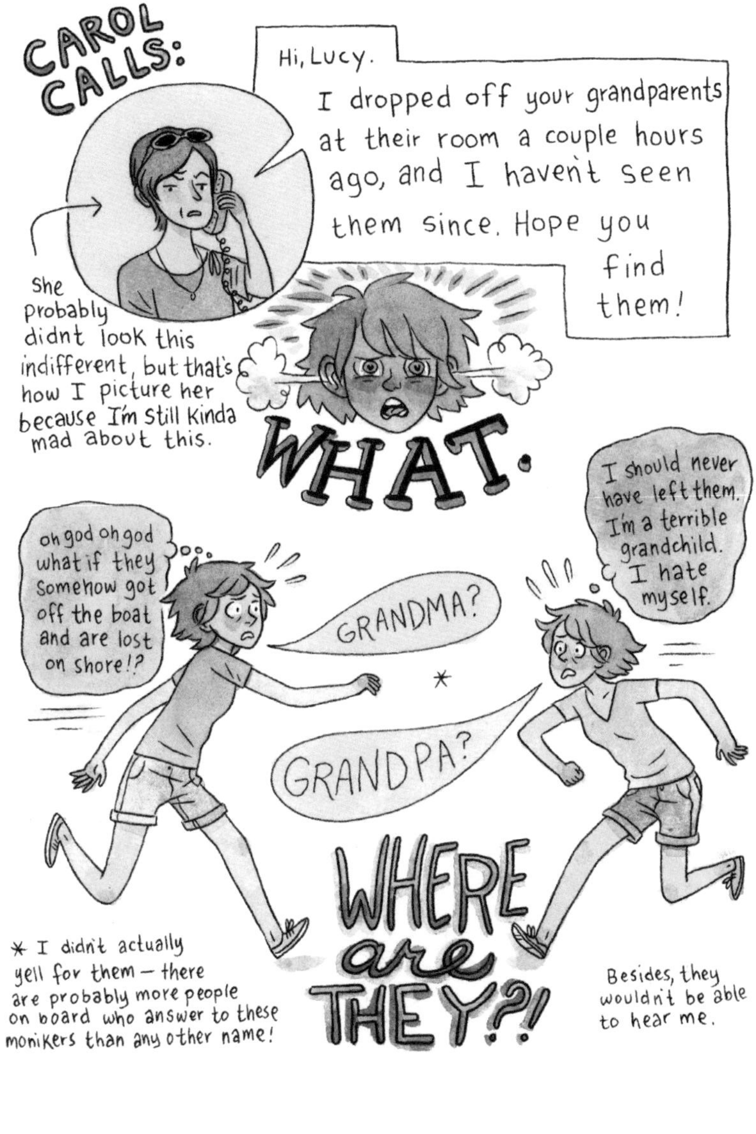
CAROL CALLS:
Hi, Lucy.
I dropped off your grandparents at their room a couple hours ago, and I haven't seen them since. Hope you find them!
She probably didnt look this indifferent, but that's how I picture her because I'm still kinda mad about this.
WHAT.
oh god oh god what if they somehow got off the boat and are lost on shore!?
I should never have left them. I'm a terrible grandchild. I hate myself.
GRANDMA?
*
GRANDPA?
WHERE are THEY?!
* I didn't actually yell for them — there are probably more people on board who answer to these monikers than any other name!
Besides, they wouldn't be able to hear me.

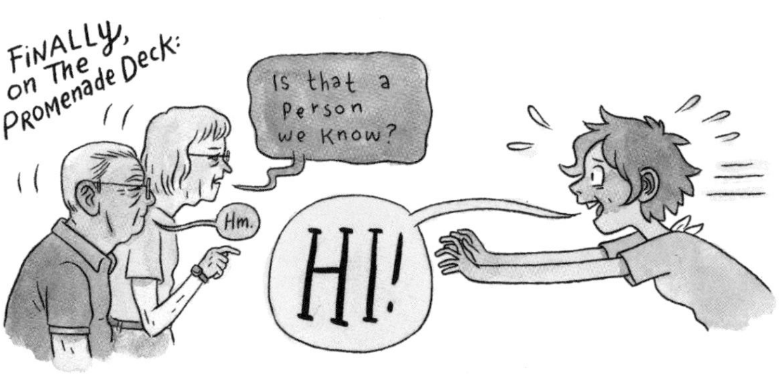
FINALLY, on The Promenade Deck:
Is that a person we know?
Hm.
HI!

They'd just been *WANDERING* around, looking for something recognizable.

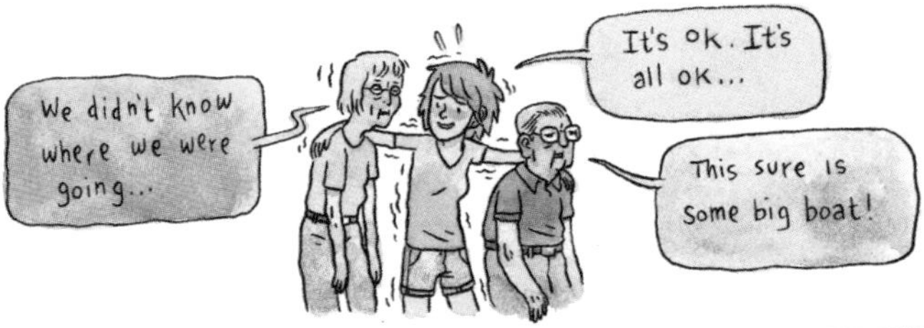
We didn't know where we were going...
It's ok. It's all ok...
This sure is some big boat!

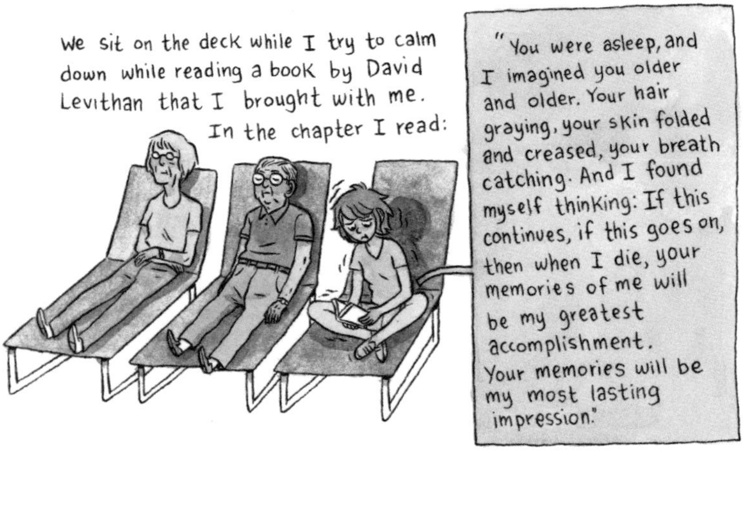
We sit on the deck while I try to calm down while reading a book by David Levithan that I brought with me. In the chapter I read:
"You were asleep, and I imagined you older and older. Your hair graying, your skin folded and creased, your breath catching. And I found myself thinking: If this continues, if this goes on, then when I die, your memories of me will be my greatest accomplishment. Your memories will be my most lasting impression."

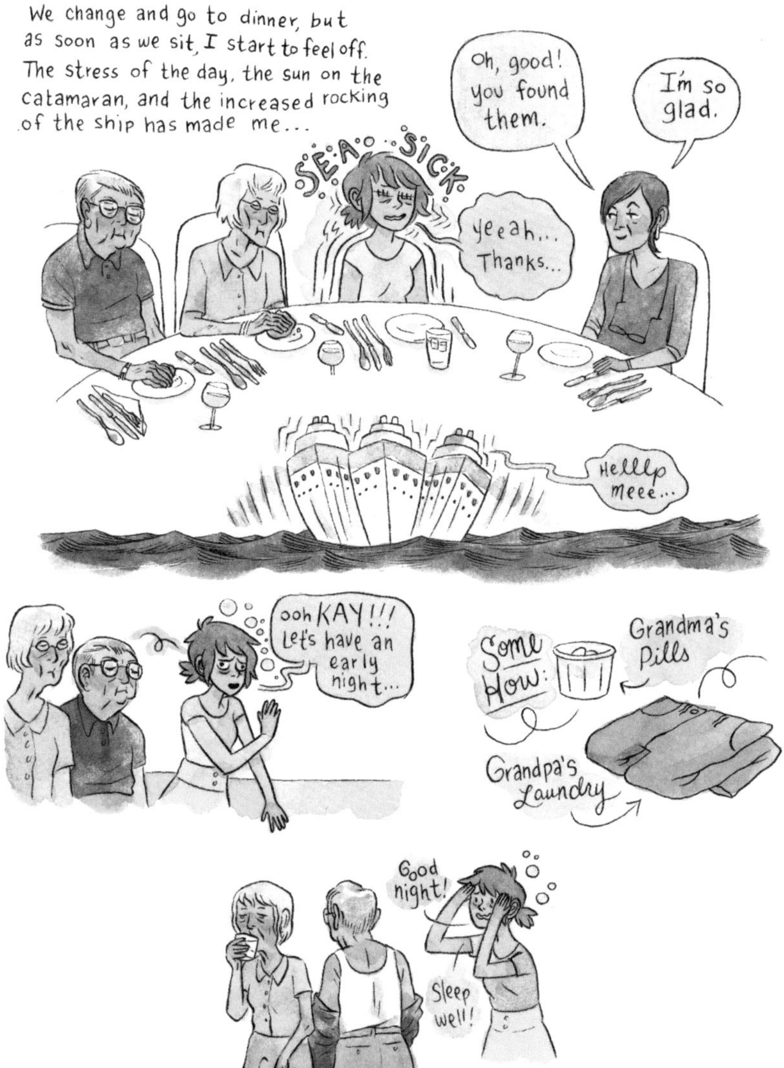
We change and go to dinner, but as soon as we sit, I start to feel off. The stress of the day, the sun on the catamaran, and the increased rocking of the ship has made me...
SEA SICK
Oh, good! you found them.
I'm so glad.
yeeah... Thanks...
Helllp meee...
oohKAY!!! Let's have an early night...
Some How:
Grandma's Pills
Grandpa's Laundry
Good night!
Sleep well!

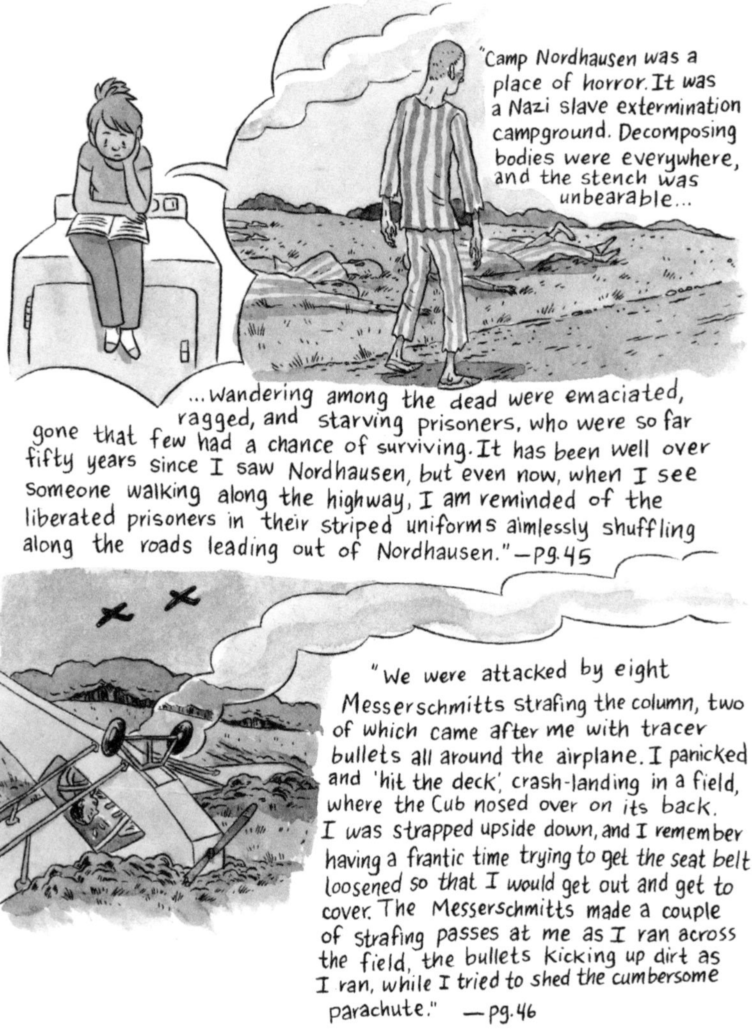
"Camp Nordhausen was a place of horror. It was a Nazi slave extermination campground. Decomposing bodies were everywhere, and the stench was unbearable...
...wandering among the dead were emaciated, ragged, and starving prisoners, who were so far gone that few had a chance of surviving. It has been well over fifty years since I saw Nordhausen, but even now, when I see someone walking along the highway, I am reminded of the liberated prisoners in their striped uniforms aimlessly shuffling along the roads leading out of Nordhausen." —pg.45
"We were attacked by eight Messerschmitts strafing the column, two of which came after me with tracer bullets all around the airplane. I panicked and 'hit the deck', crash-landing in a field, where the Cub nosed over on its back. I was strapped upside down, and I remember having a frantic time trying to get the seat belt loosened so that I would get out and get to cover. The Messerschmitts made a couple of strafing passes at me as I ran across the field, the bullets kicking up dirt as I ran, while I tried to shed the cumbersome parachute." —pg.46

This Cruise is A Metaphor for Mortality

The whole world is rocking back and forth.

Day 8

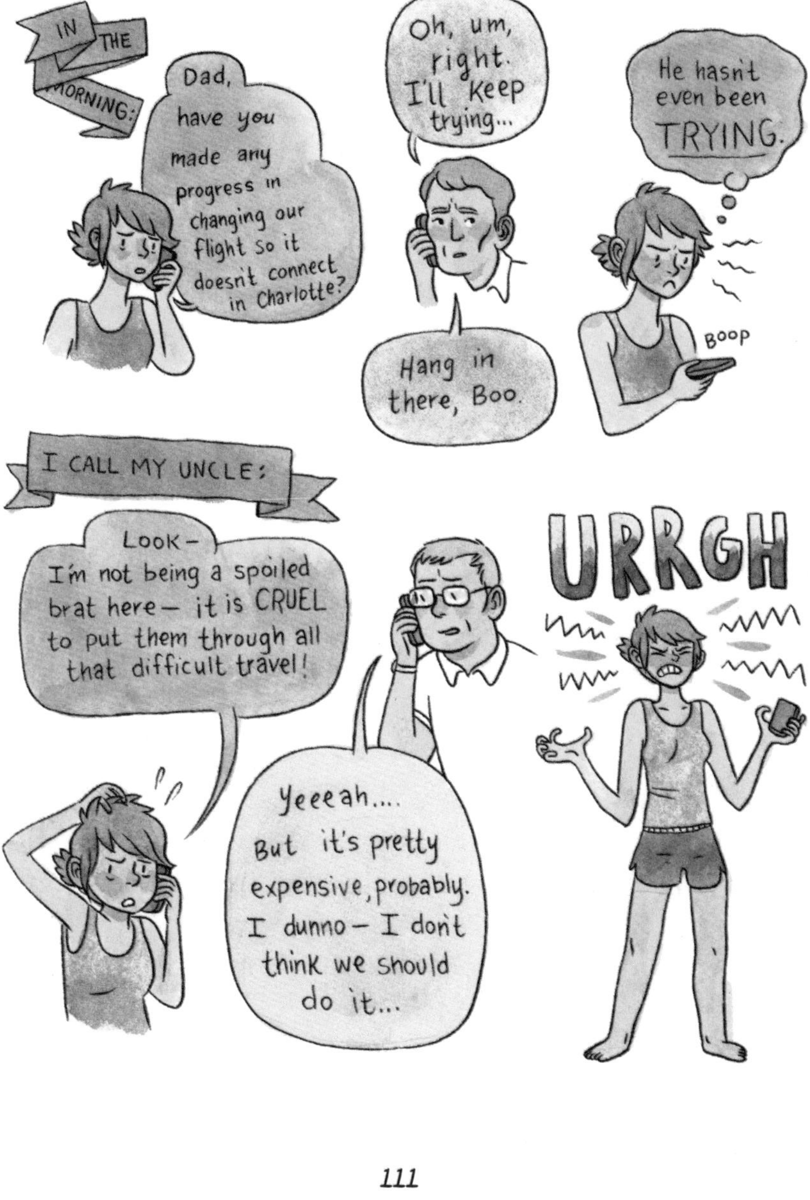
IN THE MORNING:
Dad, have you made any progress in changing our flight so it doesn't connect in Charlotte?
Oh, um, right. I'll keep trying...
Hang in there, Boo.
He hasn't even been TRYING.
BOOP
I CALL MY UNCLE:
Look– I'm not being a spoiled brat here– it is CRUEL to put them through all that difficult travel!
Yeeeah.... But it's pretty expensive, probably. I dunno– I don't think we should do it...
URRGH

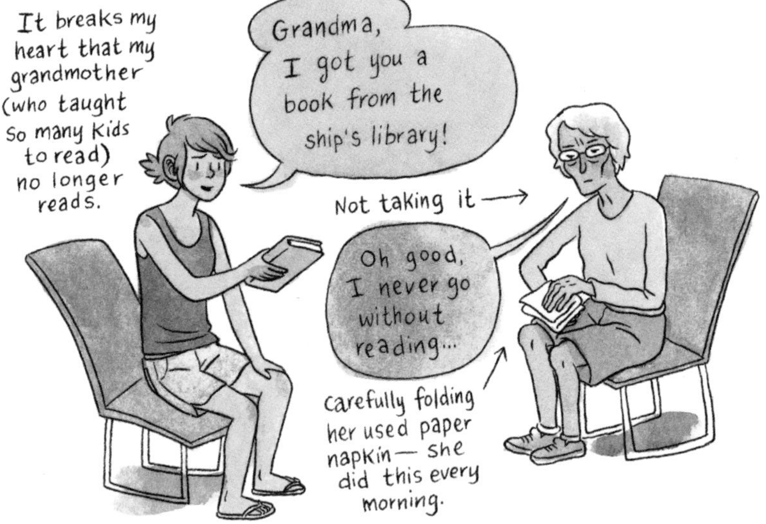

It breaks my heart that my grandmother (who taught so many kids to read) no longer reads.
Grandma, I got you a book from the ship's library!
Not taking it →
Oh good, I never go without reading...
carefully folding her used paper napkin— she did this every morning.

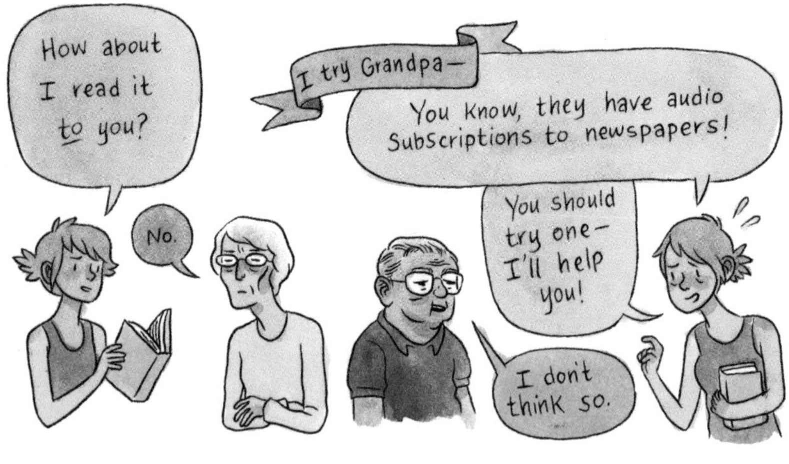

How about I read it to you?
No.
I try Grandpa—
You know, they have audio subscriptions to newspapers!
You should try one— I'll help you!
I don't think so.

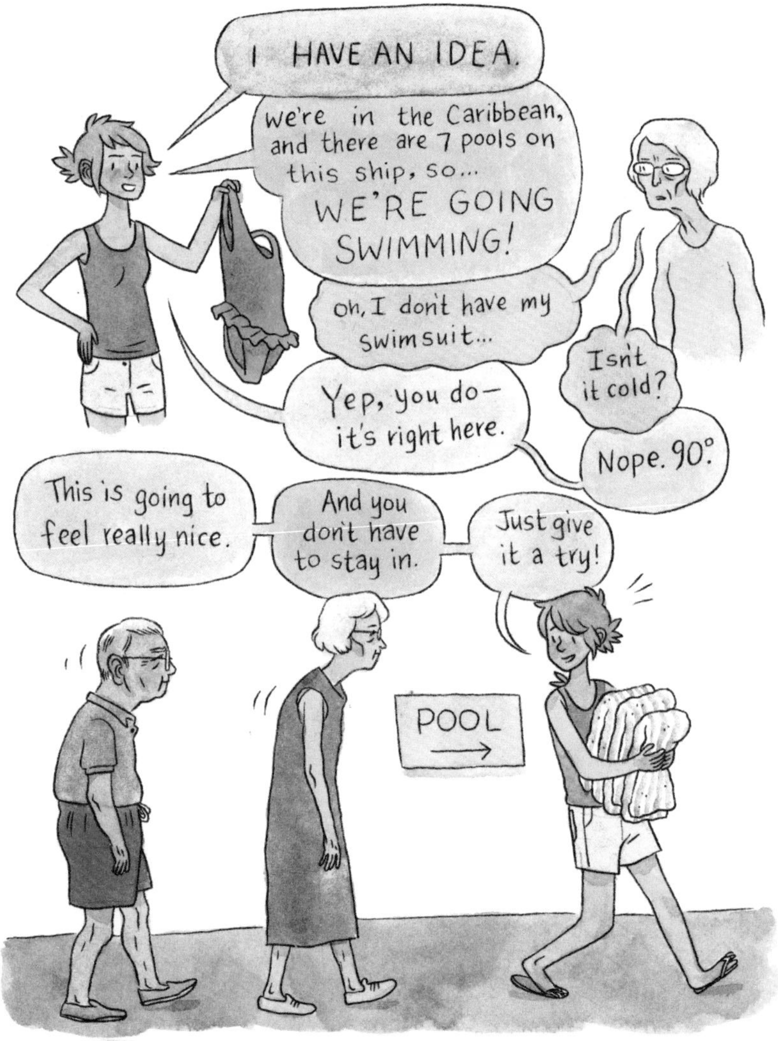
I HAVE AN IDEA.
We're in the Caribbean, and there are 7 pools on this ship, so... WE'RE GOING SWIMMING!
Oh, I don't have my swimsuit...
Yep, you do— it's right here.
Isn't it cold?
Nope. 90°
This is going to feel really nice.
And you don't have to stay in.
Just give it a try!
POOL

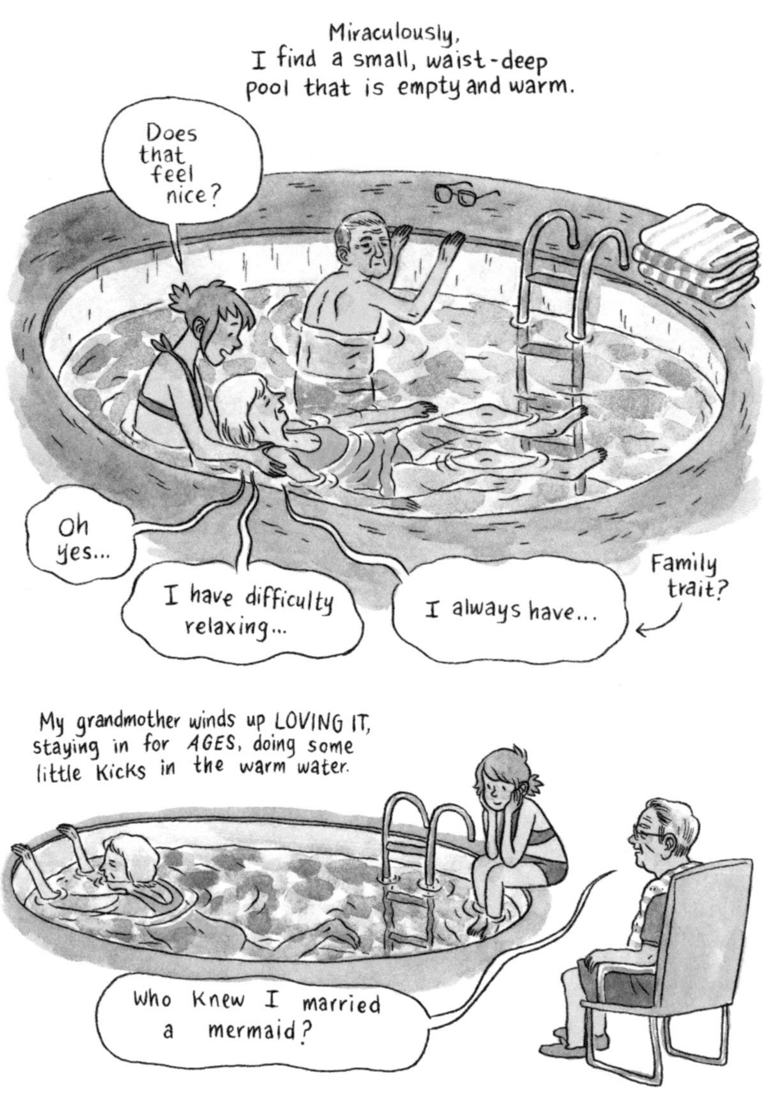
Miraculously, I find a small, waist-deep pool that is empty and warm.
Does that feel nice?
Oh yes...
I have difficulty relaxing...
I always have...
Family trait?
My grandmother winds up LOVING IT, staying in for AGES, doing some little Kicks in the warm water.
Who Knew I married a mermaid?

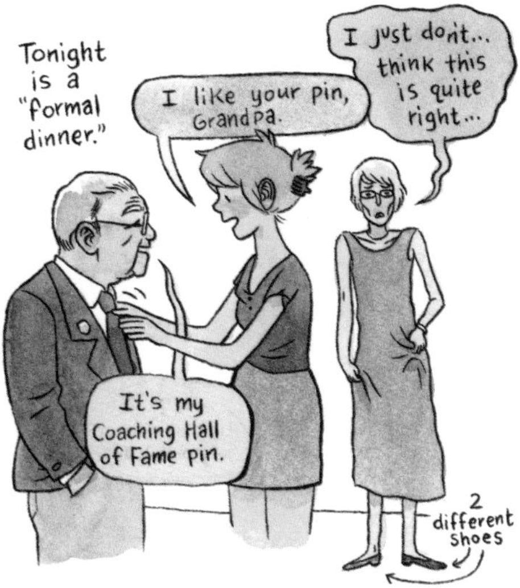
Tonight is a "formal dinner."
I like your pin, Grandpa.
I just don't... think this is quite right...
It's my Coaching Hall of Fame pin.
2 different shoes

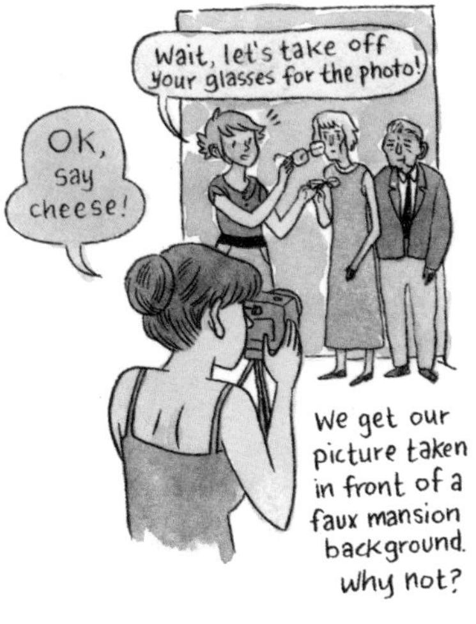
Wait, let's take off your glasses for the photo!
OK, say cheese!
We get our picture taken in front of a faux mansion background. Why not?

Talking at dinner to Nancy, a retired nurse.

We only got the one photo — Grandma has a bad corn,* so she has trouble standing in her fancy shoes.

Have you ever considered nursing?

You're so good with your grandparents!

*What exactly is a "corn"?

Frankly, this whole trip has given me a new respect and awe for caretakers.

Thanks!

But I doubt I'd be as good with people I'm not related to!

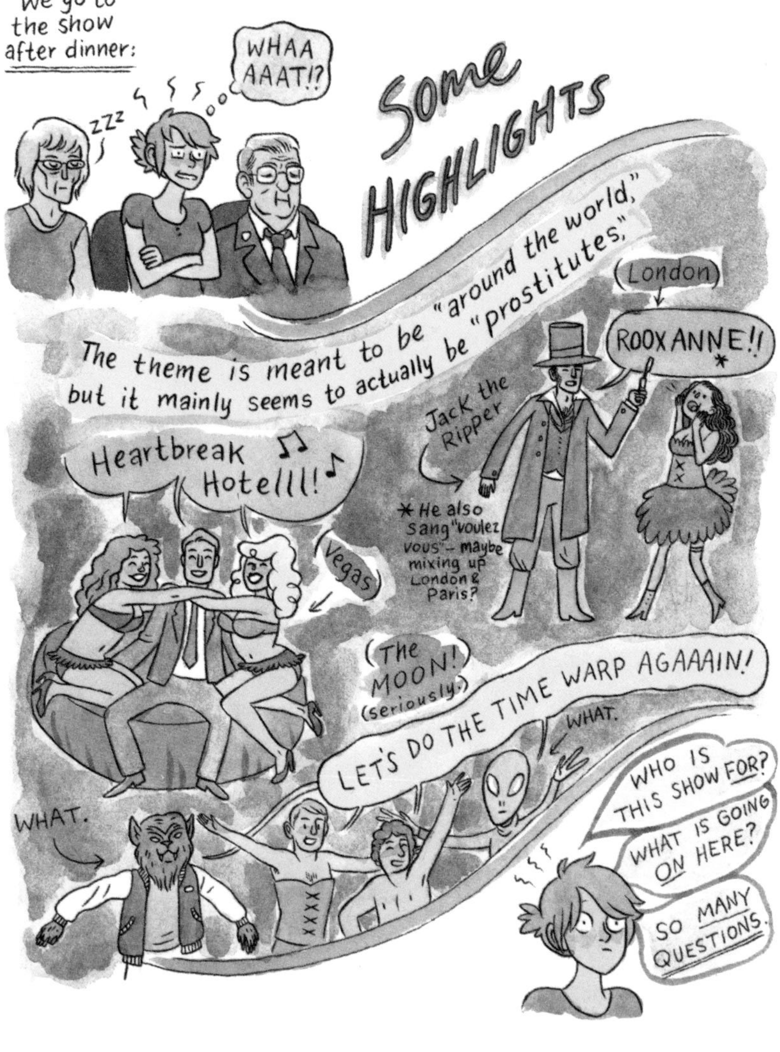

We go to the show after dinner:
ZZZ
WHAA AAAT!?
Some HIGHLIGHTS
The theme is meant to be "around the world," but it mainly seems to actually be "prostitutes."
London
ROOXANNE!! *
Jack the Ripper
Heartbreak Hotelll!
* He also sang "voulez vous" - maybe mixing up London & Paris?
Vegas
(The MOON! (seriously.)
LET'S DO THE TIME WARP AGAAAIN!
WHAT.
WHAT.
WHO IS THIS SHOW FOR?
WHAT IS GOING ON HERE?
SO MANY QUESTIONS.

Evening Meds Time

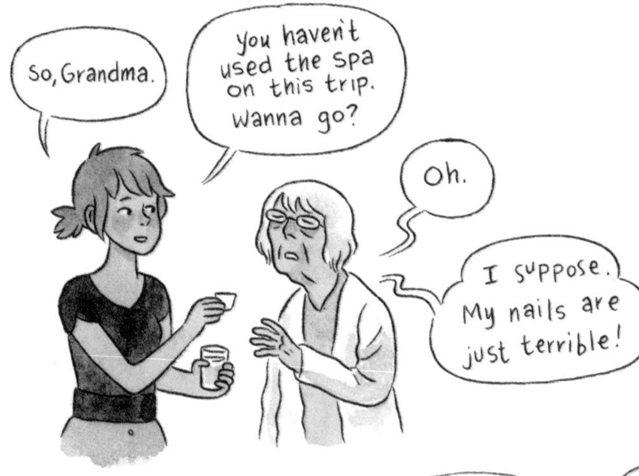
So, Grandma.
You haven't used the spa on this trip. Wanna go?
Oh.
I suppose. My nails are just terrible!

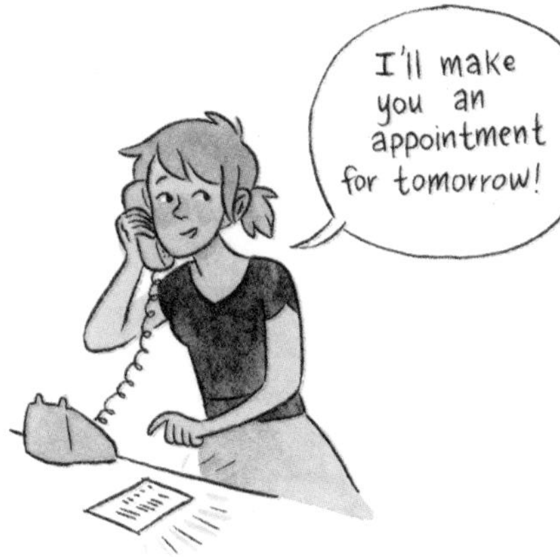
I'll make you an appointment for tomorrow!

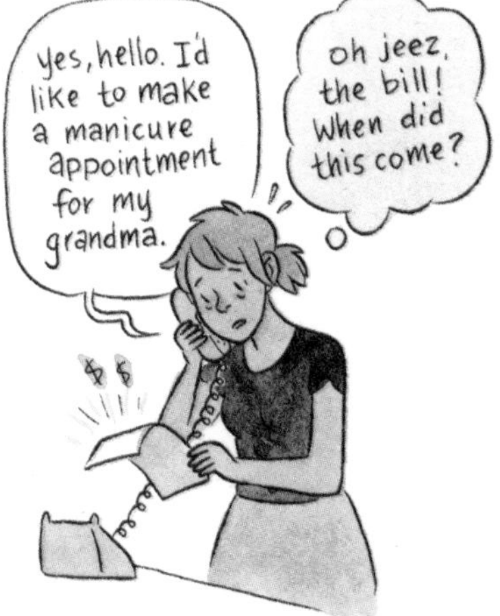
Yes, hello. I'd like to make a manicure appointment for my grandma.
Oh jeez, the bill! When did this come?
$ $

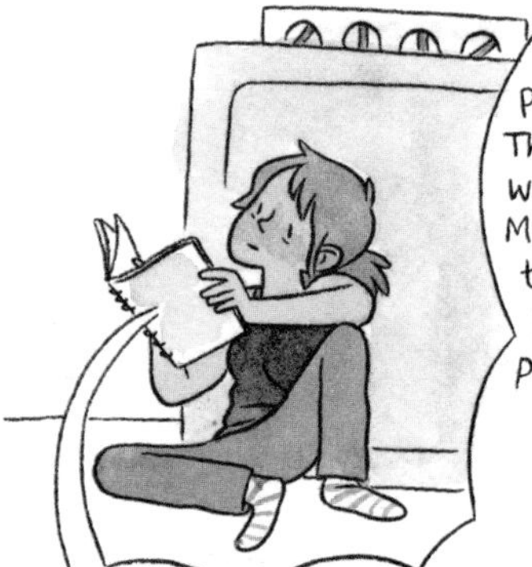

"I was in Casablanca a couple of days, then left on August 5th on a C54 transport plane for Miami, Florida, with three stops. The first thing I did, after landing in Miami, was to call Phyllis, who was working in Manhattan and living in Brooklyn. We arranged to meet in Grand Central Station. Japan had yet to surrender, but we decided to make plans to be married on August 26th.

We spent our honeymoon trip on a smoky, dirty, hot train ride from Columbus to Harrisburg, Pennsylvania, while I argued at length with a hawk-nosed W.A.C. who insisted I sign up for the Reserves. I had had all the army I could stand and just wanted to get on with my life as a civilian.

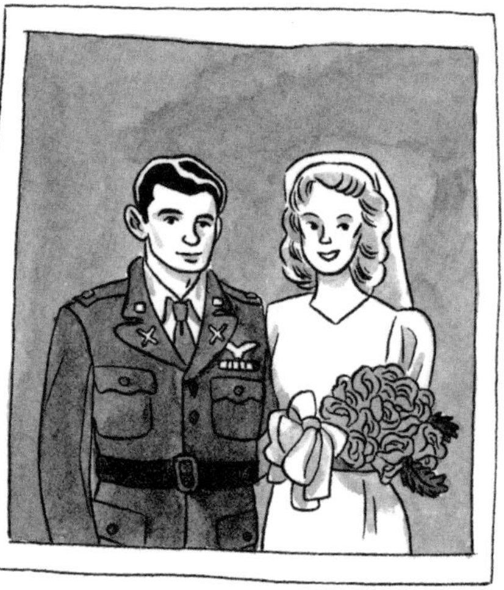

The truth is, I was never a very good soldier. Survival was always my main concern. And survival meant a lot of luck and a "live for now" philosophy. To keep my sanity in the uncertainty of combat, I think I adopted a kind of nonchalant fatalism and, as with a lot of other soldiers, the inbred senses of decency and morality were temporarily suspended."

—pg.48

Day 9

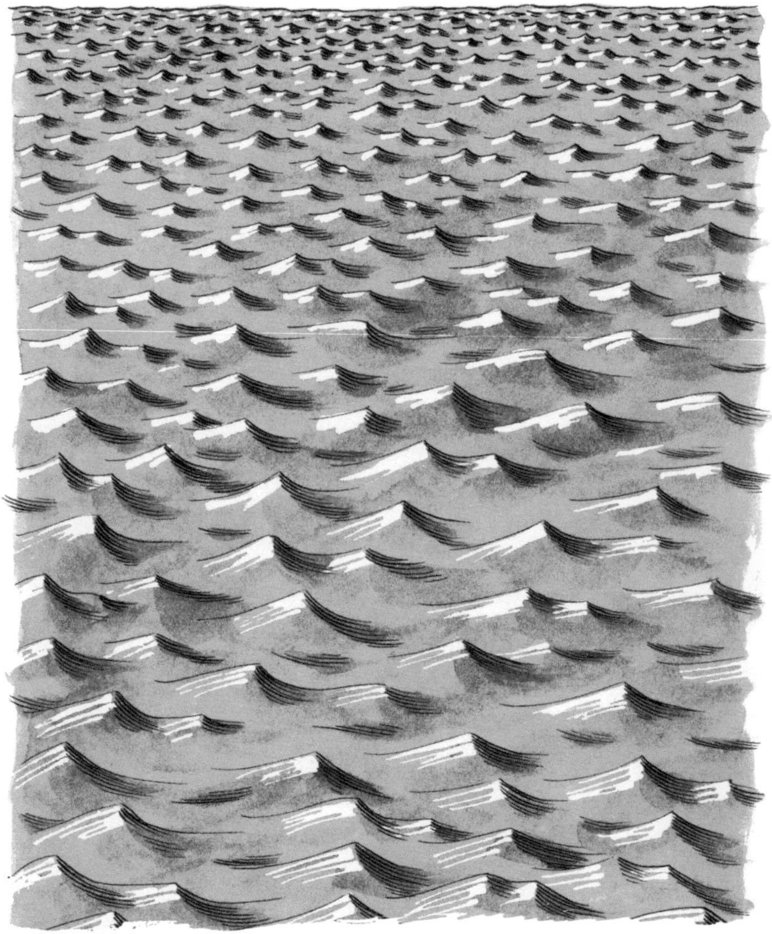

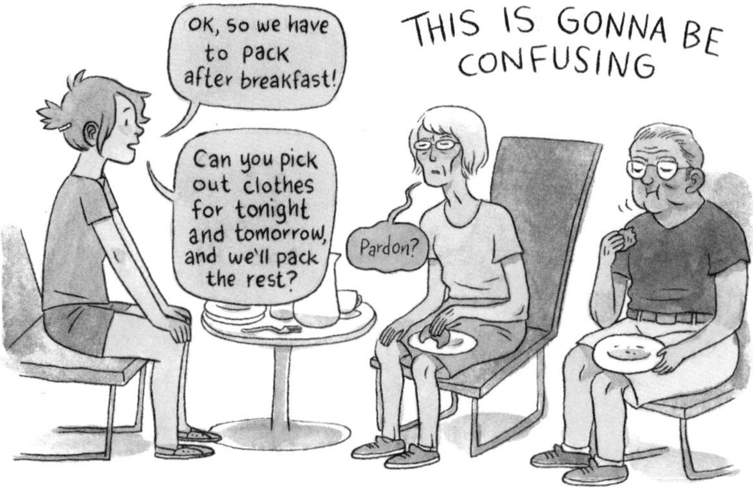
OK, so we have to pack after breakfast!
THIS IS GONNA BE CONFUSING
Can you pick out clothes for tonight and tomorrow, and we'll pack the rest?
Pardon?

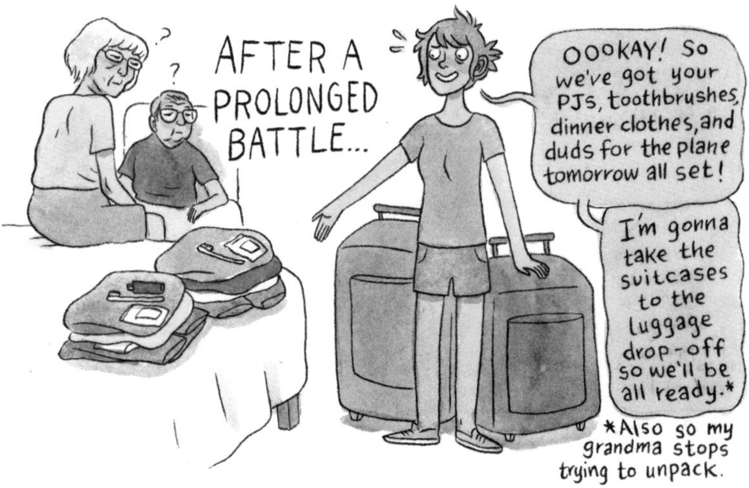
AFTER A PROLONGED BATTLE...
?
?
OOOKAY! So we've got your PJs, toothbrushes, dinner clothes, and duds for the plane tomorrow all set!
I'm gonna take the suitcases to the luggage drop-off so we'll be all ready.*
*Also so my grandma stops trying to unpack.

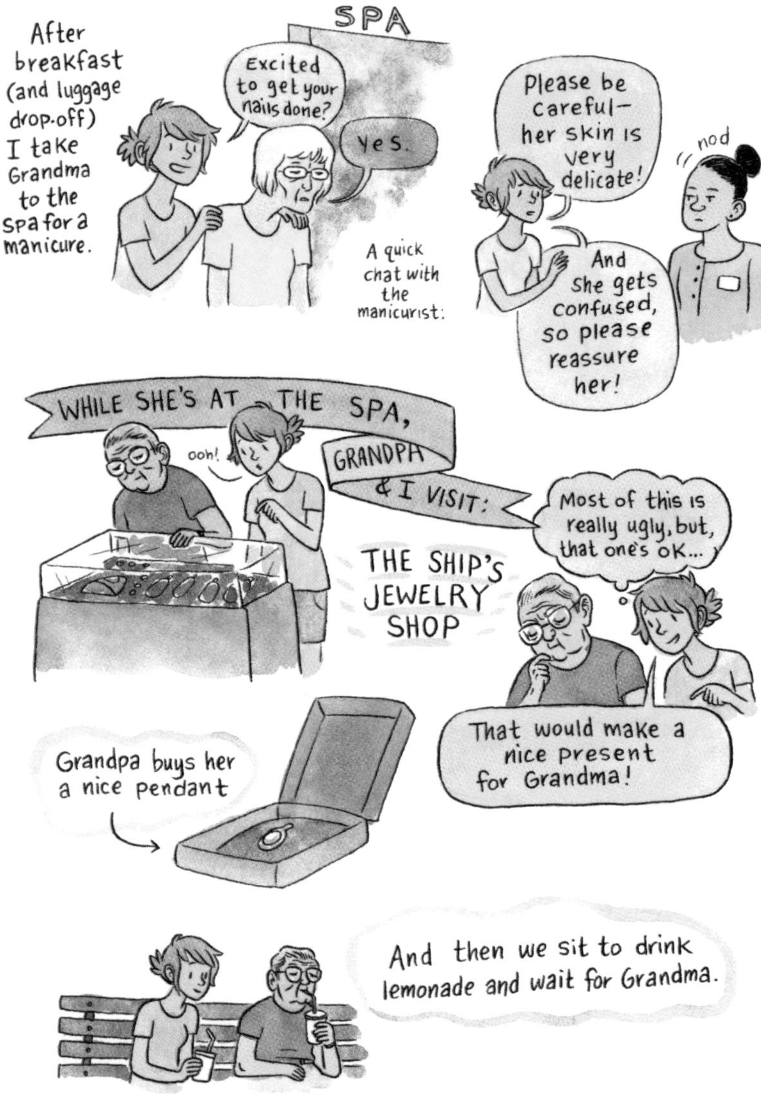
SPA
After breakfast (and luggage drop-off) I take Grandma to the spa for a manicure.
Excited to get your nails done?
Yes.
A quick chat with the manicurist:
Please be careful— her skin is very delicate!
nod
And she gets confused, so please reassure her!
WHILE SHE'S AT THE SPA, GRANDPA & I VISIT:
ooh!
THE SHIP'S JEWELRY SHOP
Most of this is really ugly, but, that one's OK...
That would make a nice present for Grandma!
Grandpa buys her a nice pendant
And then we sit to drink lemonade and wait for Grandma.

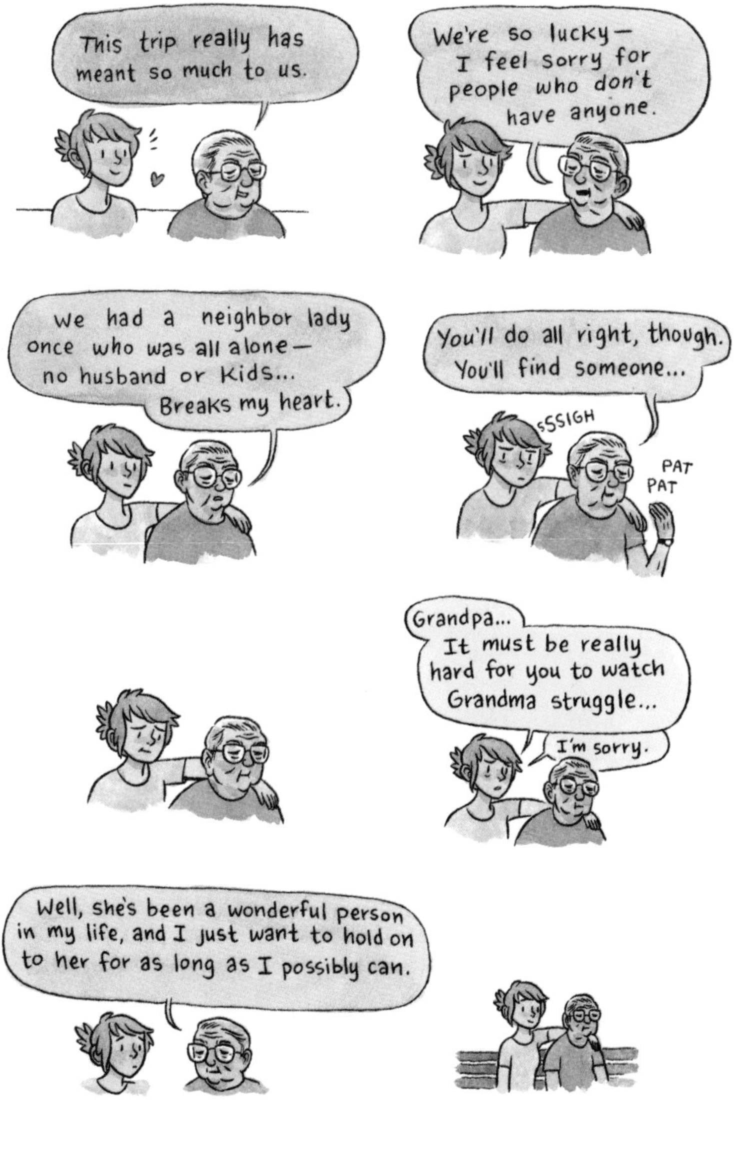
This trip really has meant so much to us.
We're so lucky— I feel sorry for people who don't have anyone.
We had a neighbor lady once who was all alone— no husband or kids...
Breaks my heart.
You'll do all right, though. You'll find someone...
SSSIGH
PAT PAT
Grandpa...
It must be really hard for you to watch Grandma struggle...
I'm sorry.
Well, she's been a wonderful person in my life, and I just want to hold on to her for as long as I possibly can.

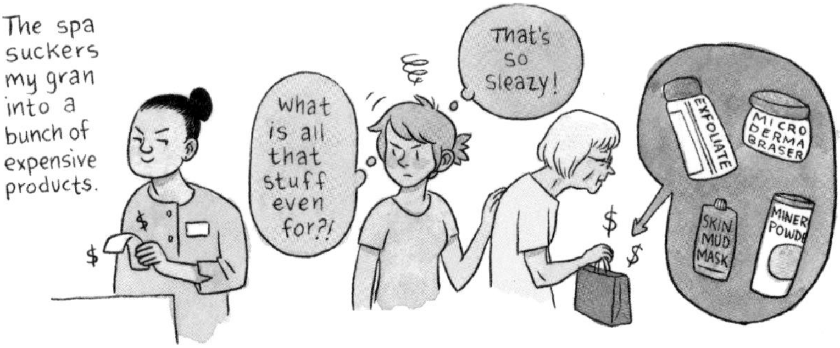
The spa suckers my gran into a bunch of expensive products.
What is all that stuff even for?!
That's so sleazy!
EXFOLIATE
MICRO DERMA BRASER
SKIN MUD MASK
MINER POWD

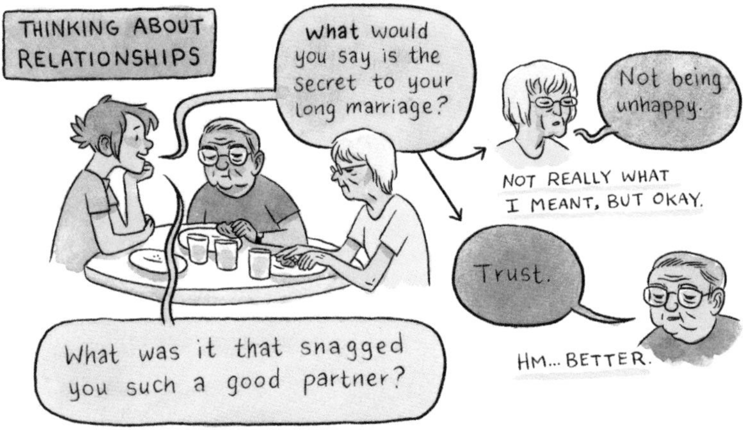
THINKING ABOUT RELATIONSHIPS
What would you say is the secret to your long marriage?
Not being unhappy.
NOT REALLY WHAT I MEANT, BUT OKAY.
Trust.
HM... BETTER.
What was it that snagged you such a good partner?

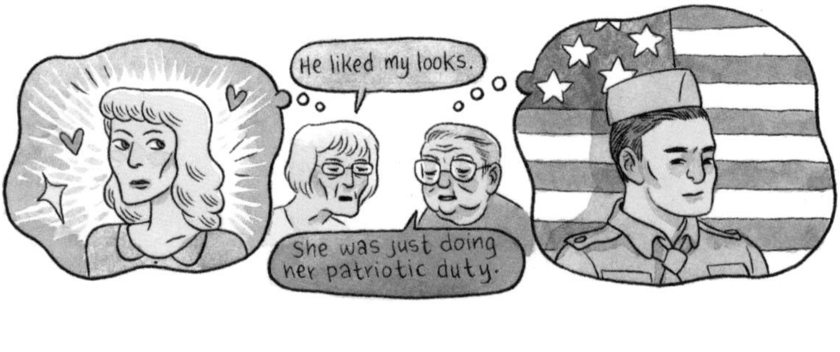
He liked my looks.
She was just doing her patriotic duty.

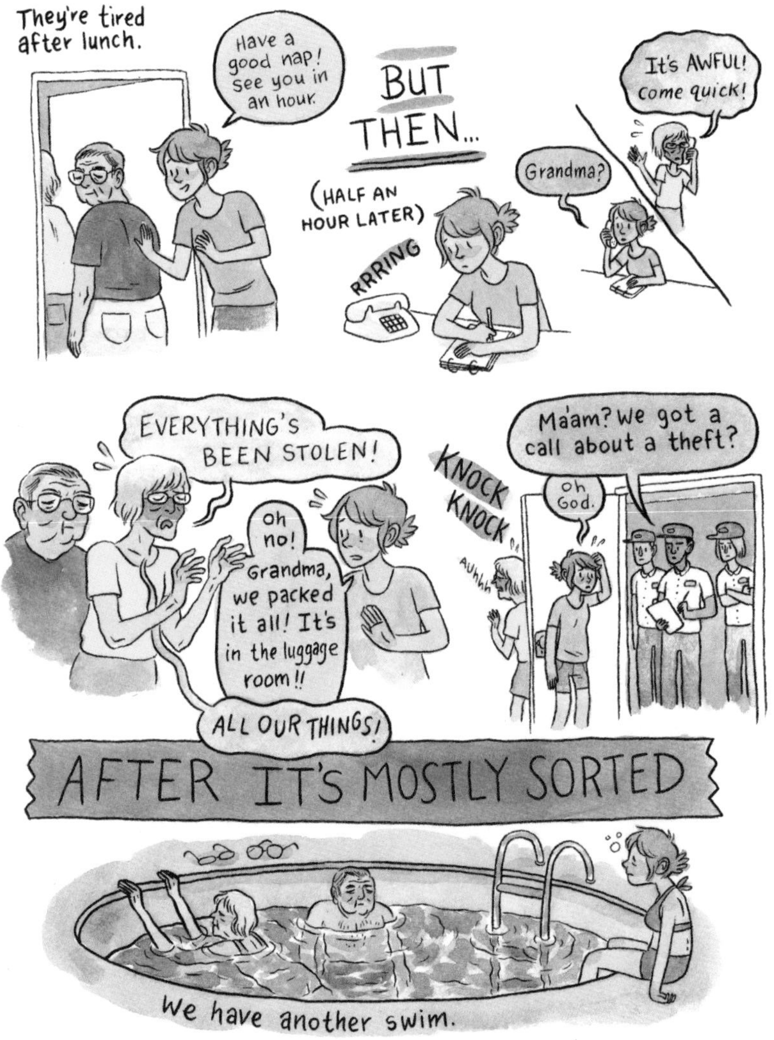
They're tired after lunch.
Have a good nap! See you in an hour.
BUT THEN...
(HALF AN HOUR LATER)
RRRING
Grandma?
It's AWFUL! Come quick!
EVERYTHING'S BEEN STOLEN!
Oh no! Grandma, we packed it all! It's in the luggage room!!
ALL OUR THINGS!
KNOCK KNOCK
Ma'am? We got a call about a theft?
Oh God.
AUhhh
AFTER IT'S MOSTLY SORTED
We have another swim.

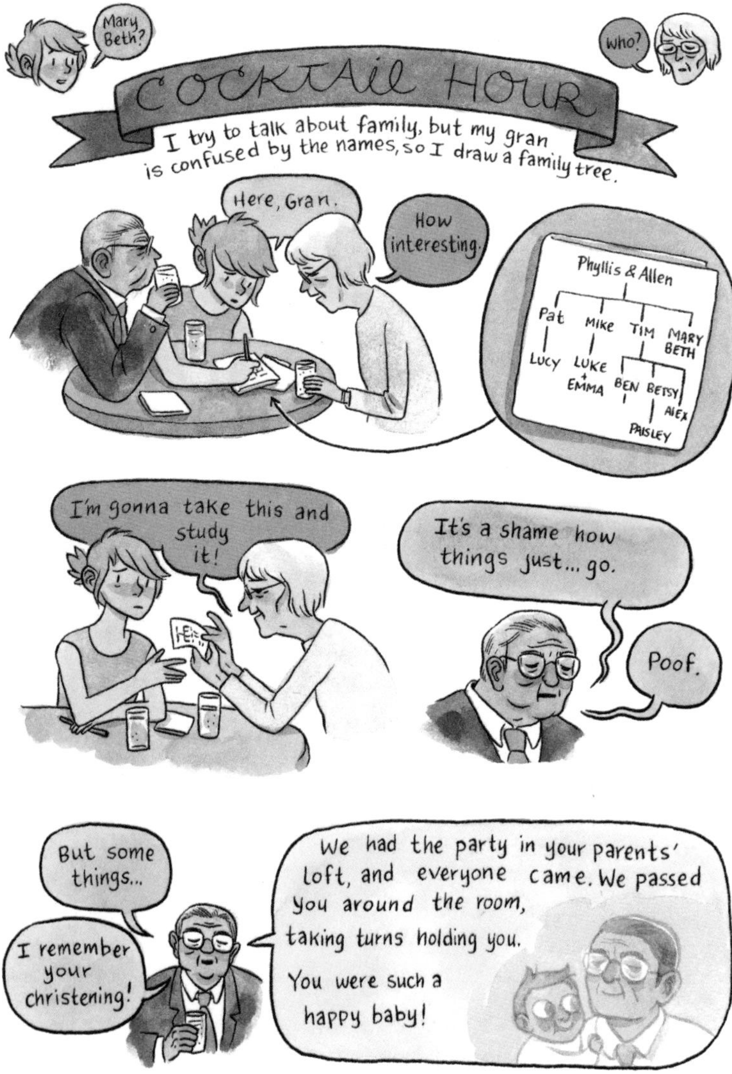
Mary Beth?
Who?
COCKTAIL HOUR
I try to talk about family, but my gran is confused by the names, so I draw a family tree.
Here, Gran.
How interesting.
Phyllis & Allen
Pat
MIKE
TIM
MARY BETH
LUCY
LUKE + EMMA
BEN
BETSY
ALEX
PAISLEY
I'm gonna take this and study it!
It's a shame how things just... go.
Poof.
But some things...
I remember your christening!
We had the party in your parents' loft, and everyone came. We passed you around the room, taking turns holding you.
You were such a happy baby!

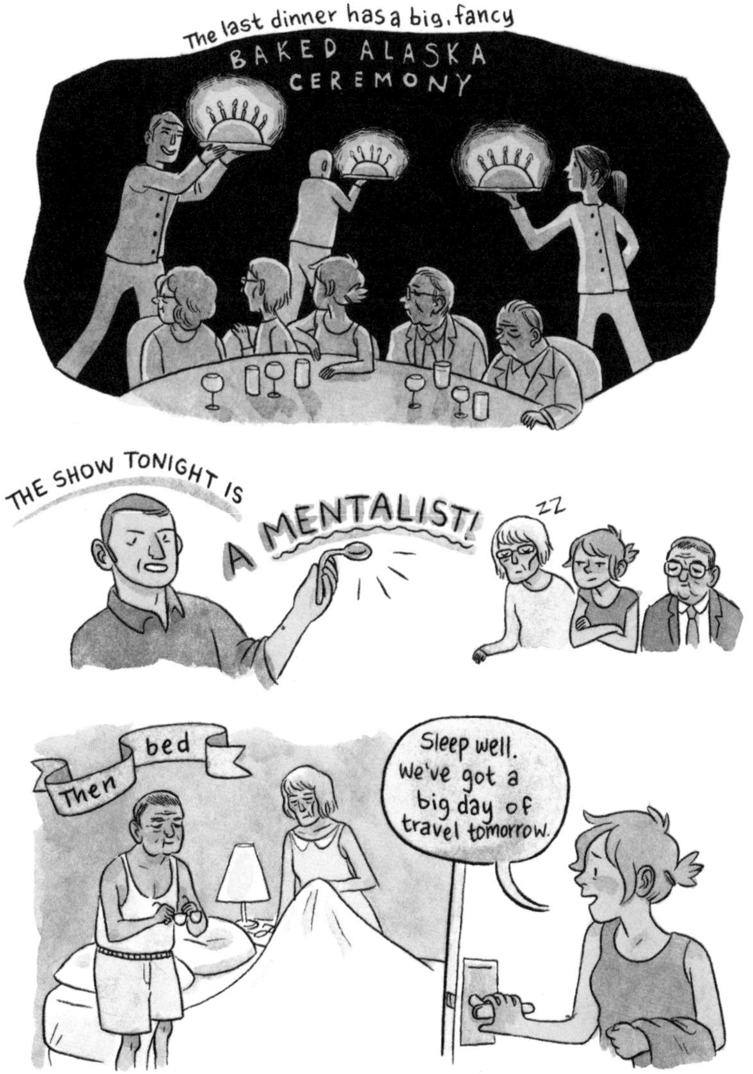
The last dinner has a big, fancy
BAKED ALASKA CEREMONY
THE SHOW TONIGHT IS
A MENTALIST!
ZZ
Then bed
Sleep well. We've got a big day of travel tomorrow.

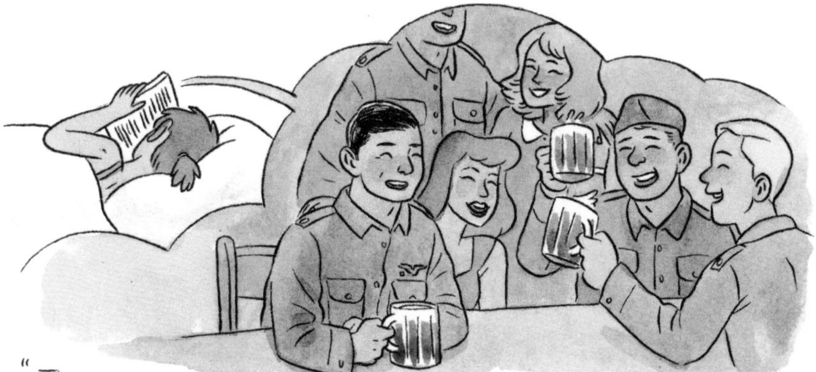

"There remain many pleasant memories. Perhaps the very uncertainty of one's future and the absence of moral restrictions during wartime enables one to enjoy life's pleasures more fully than during normal times."

—pg. 49

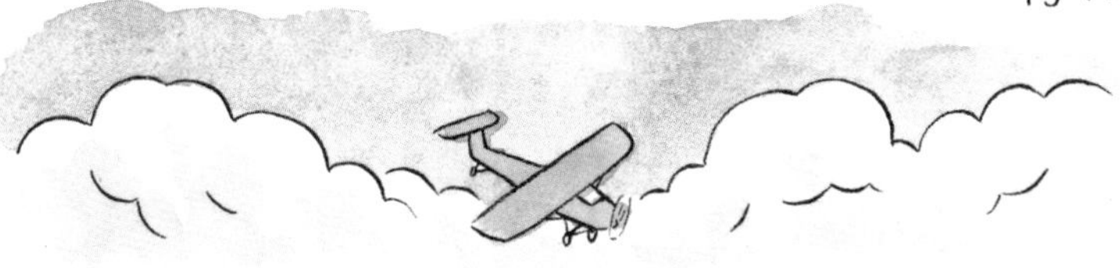

"Two big pluses of being a liaison pilot were: one, if fate decreed that I should be killed, chances were good that it would happen quickly, without the prolonged suffering that many ground troops endured. At least I would not be wading through the mud and snow, waiting for a bullet with my name on it. Secondly, from my vantage point of 500–1,000 feet above the ground operations, I could see and appreciate the "big picture" better than most people could." —pg. 49

Day 10

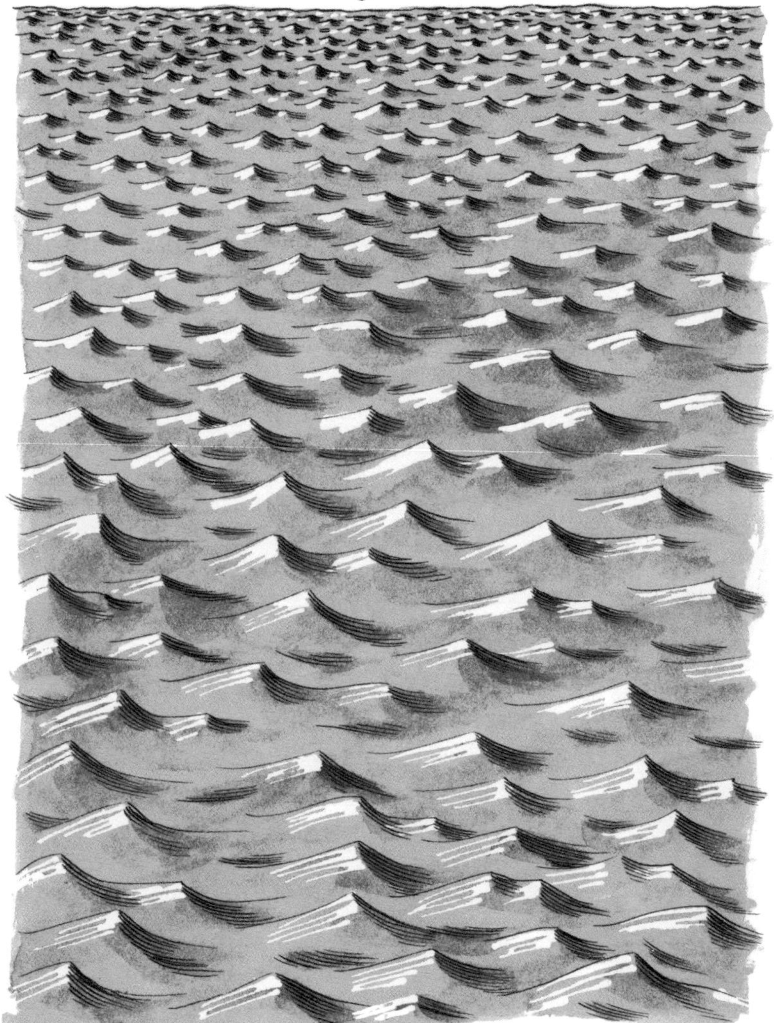

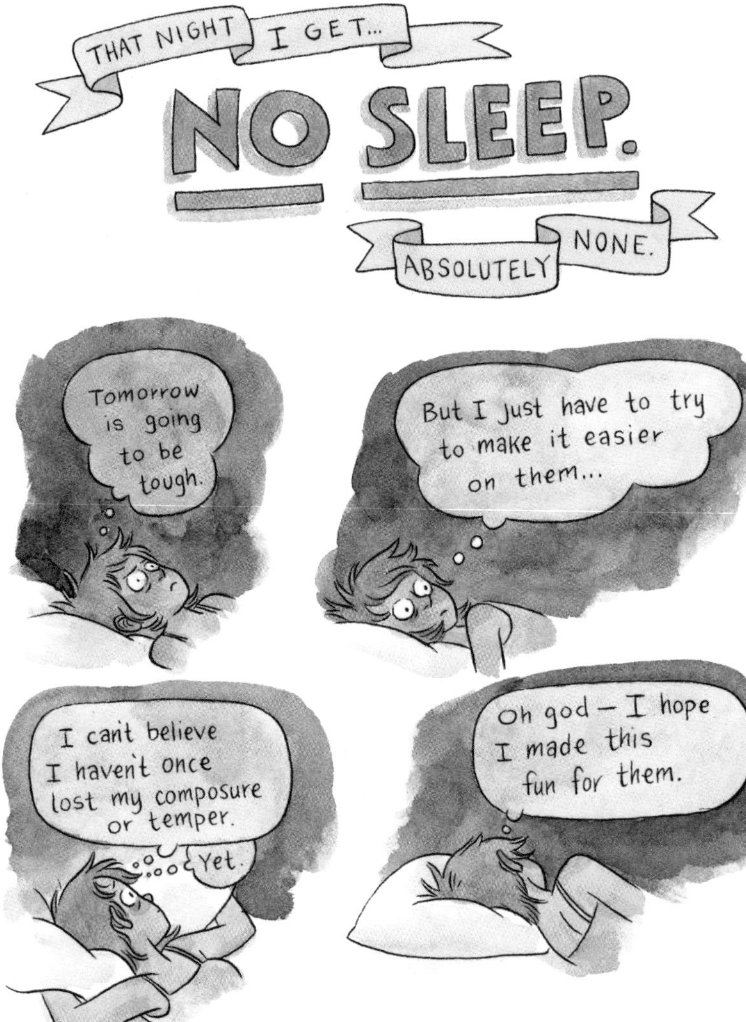
THAT NIGHT I GET...
NO SLEEP.
ABSOLUTELY NONE.
Tomorrow is going to be tough.
But I just have to try to make it easier on them...
I can't believe I haven't once lost my composure or temper.
Yet.
Oh god — I hope I made this fun for them.

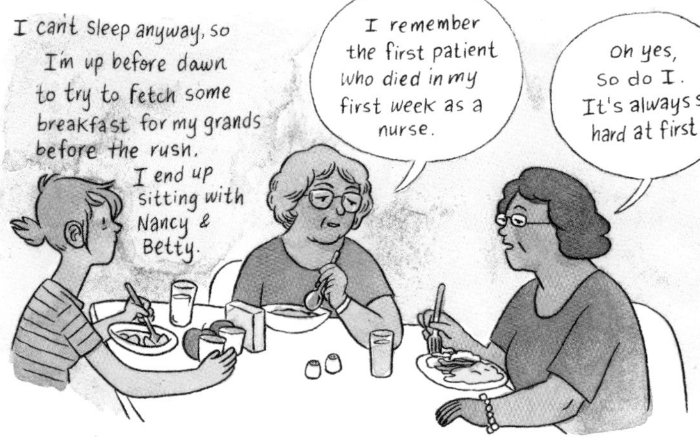
I can't sleep anyway, so I'm up before dawn to try to fetch some breakfast for my grands before the rush.
I end up sitting with Nancy & Betty.
I remember the first patient who died in my first week as a nurse.
Oh yes, so do I. It's always so hard at first.

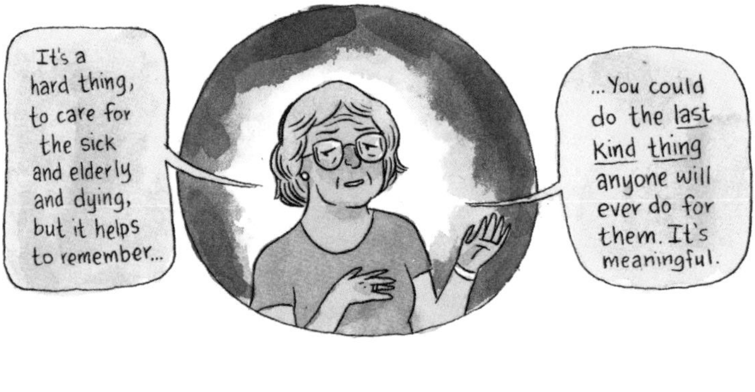
It's a hard thing, to care for the sick and elderly and dying, but it helps to remember...
...You could do the last kind thing anyone will ever do for them. It's meaningful.

On the way to bring food back to G&G, I'm stopped by our hallway custodian.

When are you and your grandparents leaving?

Oh, um. In an hour?

OK, good, because I have to do extra cleaning in your grandparents' bathroom.

I don't envy that guy, but... isn't that his job?

After breakfast:

WORRY

OK! You ready to go?

Don't worry— it's gonna be a piece of cake!

WORRY

ON THE WAY TO DISEMBARK, MY GRANDPA HAS AN

ASTHMA ATTACK

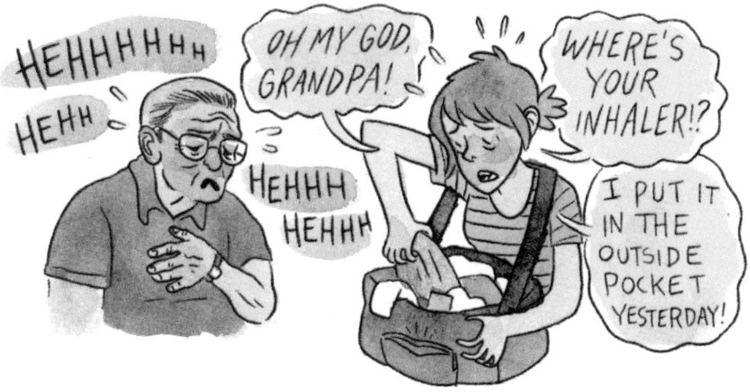
HEHHHHHH
HEHH
OH MY GOD, GRANDPA!
HEHHH
HEHHH
WHERE'S YOUR INHALER!?
I PUT IT IN THE OUTSIDE POCKET YESTERDAY!

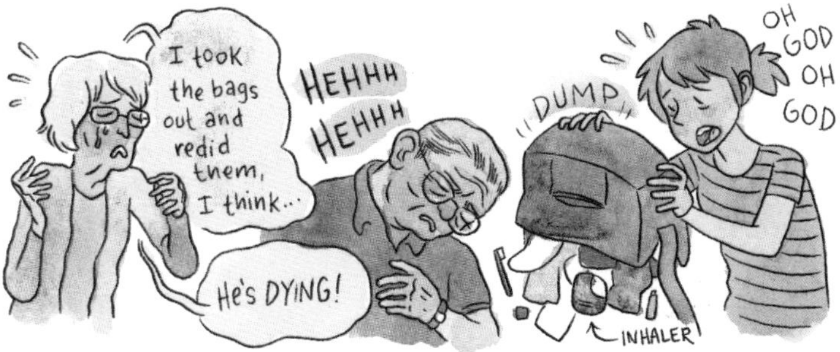
I took the bags out and redid them, I think...
He's DYING!
HEHHH
HEHHH
DUMP
OH GOD OH GOD
INHALER

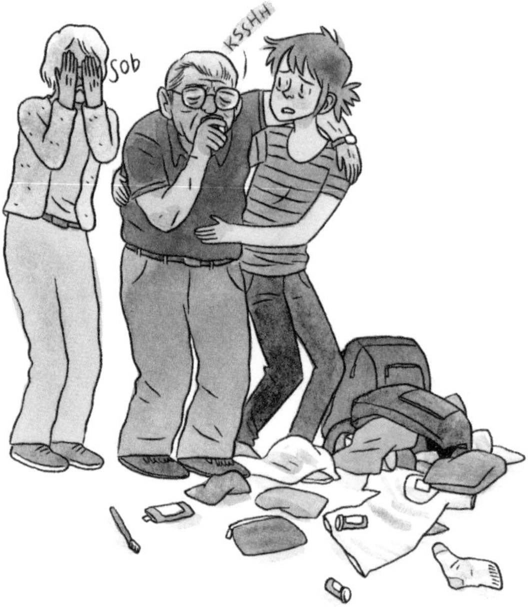
SOB
KSSHH

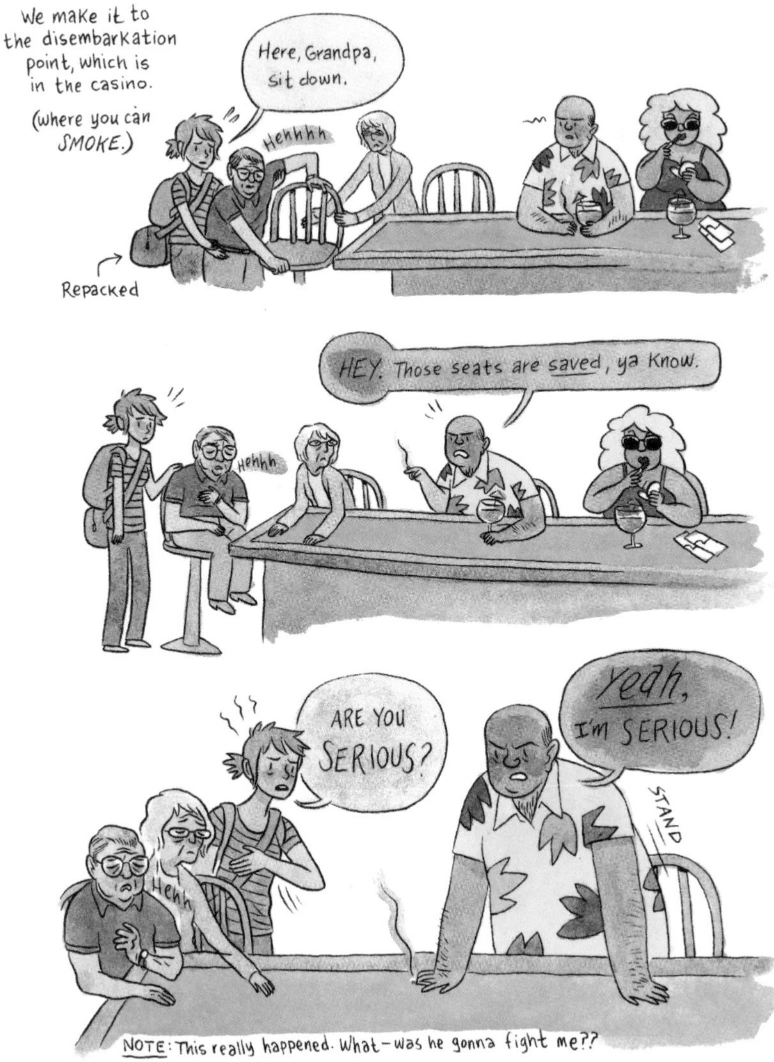
We make it to the disembarkation point, which is in the casino.
(where you can SMOKE.)
Here, Grandpa, sit down.
Hehhhh
Repacked
HEY. Those seats are saved, ya Know.
Hehhh
ARE YOU SERIOUS?
Yeah, I'm SERIOUS!
STAND
Henh
NOTE: This really happened. What—was he gonna fight me??

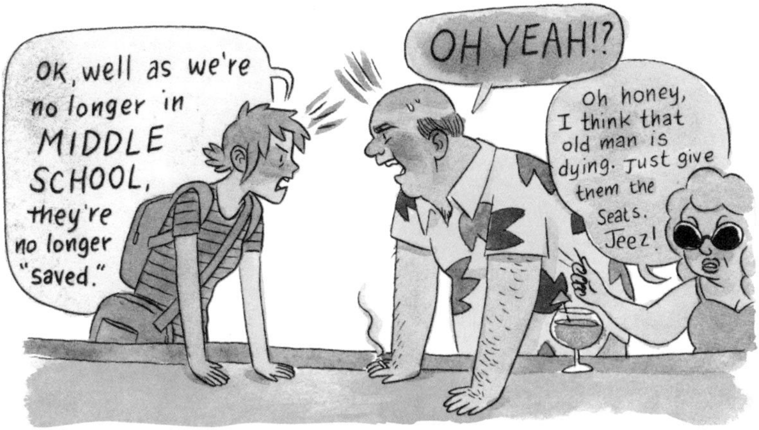
Ok, well as we're no longer in MIDDLE SCHOOL, they're no longer "saved."
OH YEAH!?
Oh honey, I think that old man is dying. Just give them the Seats. Jeez!

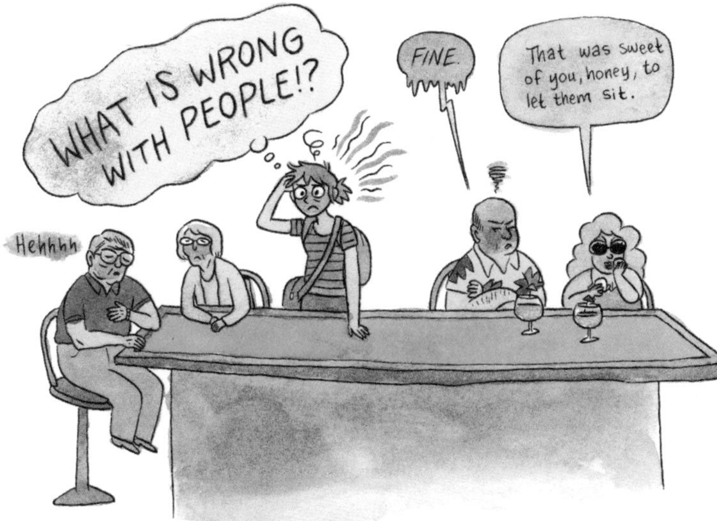
WHAT IS WRONG WITH PEOPLE!?
FINE.
That was sweet of you, honey, to let them sit.
Hehhhh

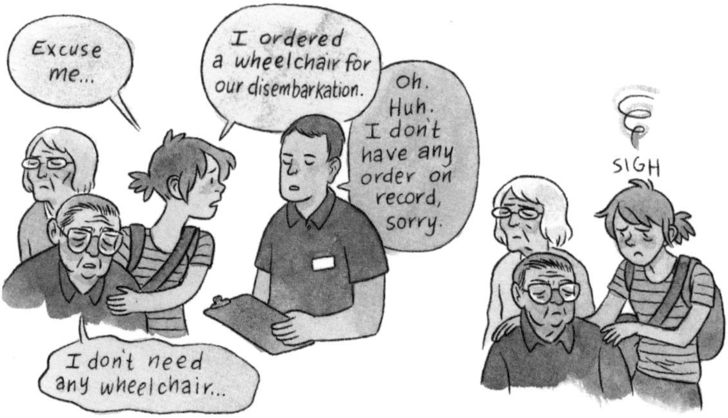
Excuse me...
I ordered a wheelchair for our disembarkation.
Oh. Huh. I don't have any order on record, sorry.
I don't need any wheelchair...
SIGH

We make it through the luggage pickup and customs without any terrible incidents, but the shuttle bus to the airport is crowded, and no one will move to let us sit together.

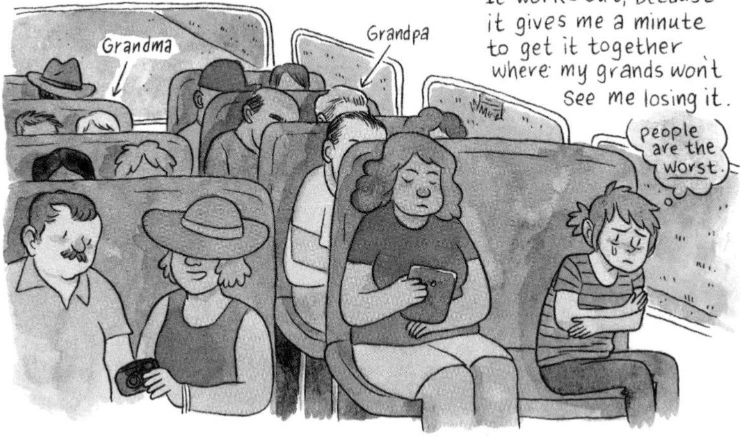
It works out, because it gives me a minute to get it together where my grands won't see me losing it.
Grandma
Grandpa
people are the worst.

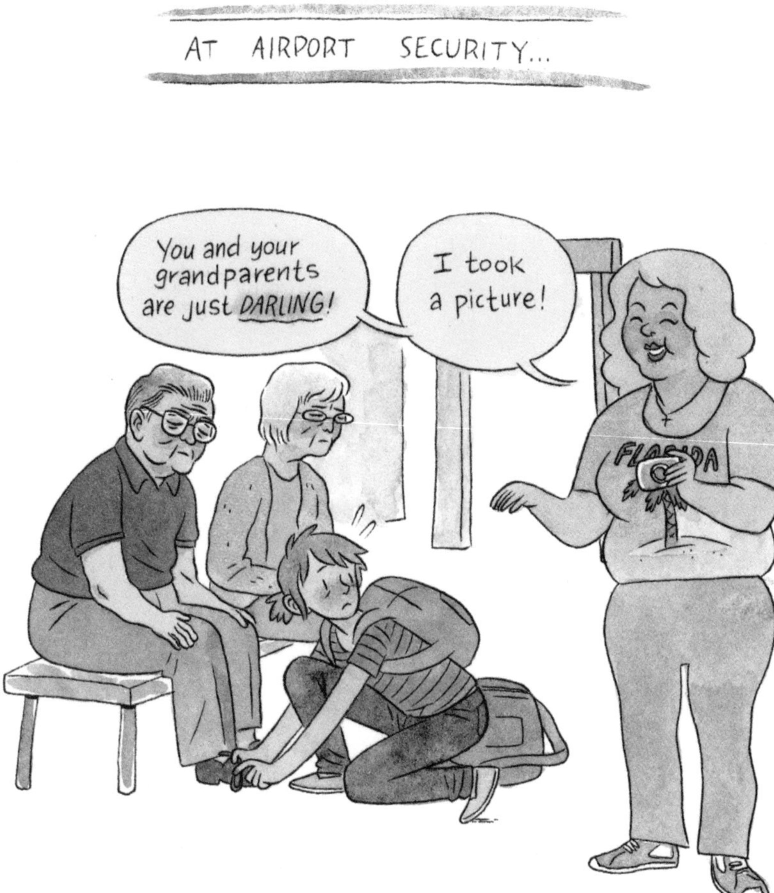
AT AIRPORT SECURITY...
You and your grandparents are just DARLING!
I took a picture!
FLORIDA

ON THE AIRPORT SHUTTLE

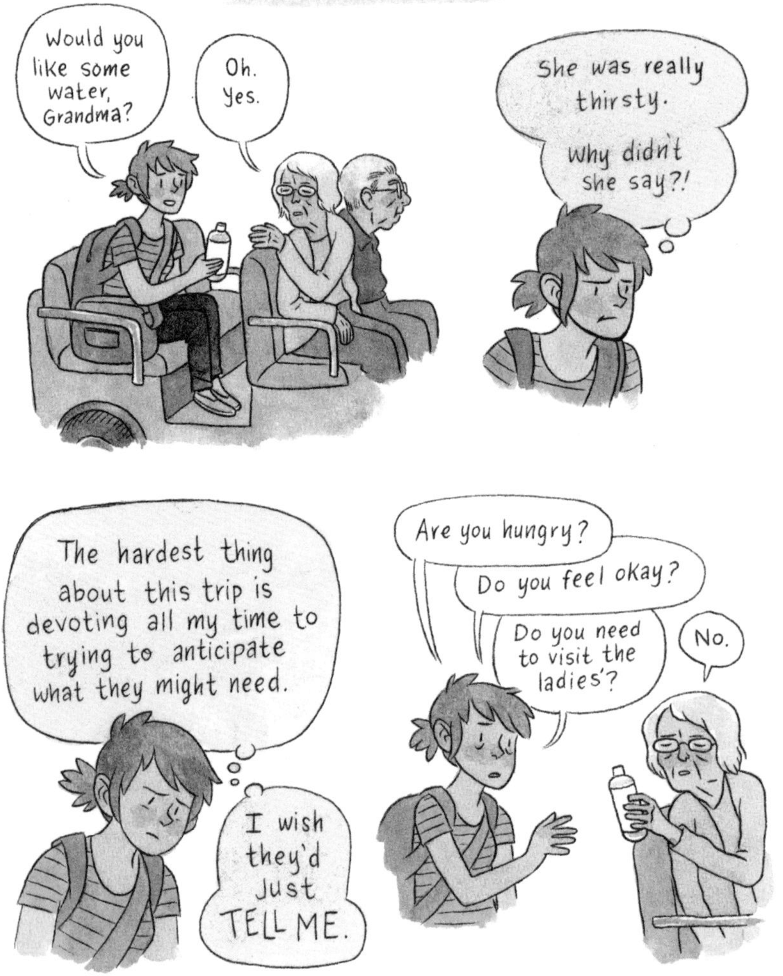
Would you like some water, Grandma?
Oh. Yes.
She was really thirsty.
Why didn't she say?!
The hardest thing about this trip is devoting all my time to trying to anticipate what they might need.
I wish they'd just TELL ME.
Are you hungry?
Do you feel okay?
Do you need to visit the ladies'?
No.

It's exhausting. Probably to everyone involved.

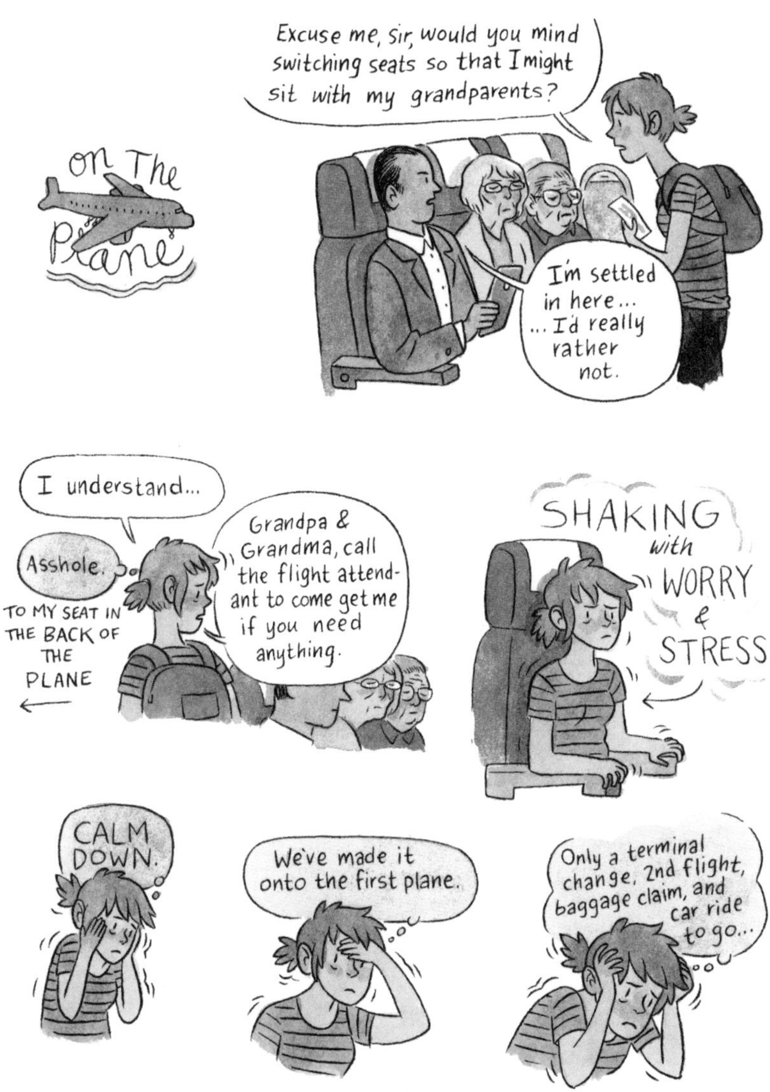
On The Plane
Excuse me, sir, would you mind switching seats so that I might sit with my grandparents?
I'm settled in here... ...I'd really rather not.
I understand...
Asshole.
Grandpa & Grandma, call the flight attendant to come get me if you need anything.
TO MY SEAT IN THE BACK OF THE PLANE
SHAKING with WORRY & STRESS
CALM DOWN.
We've made it onto the first plane.
Only a terminal change, 2nd flight, baggage claim, and car ride to go...

HALFWAY THROUGH THE FLIGHT

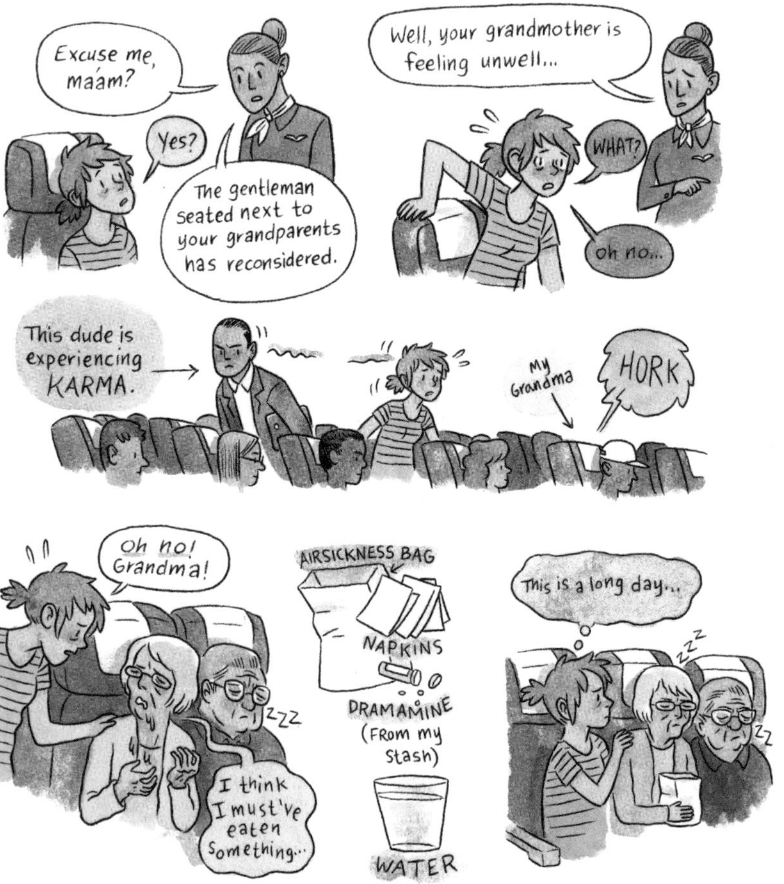

Excuse me, ma'am?
Yes?
The gentleman seated next to your grandparents has reconsidered.
Well, your grandmother is feeling unwell...
WHAT?
Oh no...
This dude is experiencing KARMA.
My Grandma
HORK
Oh no! Grandma!
I think I must've eaten something...
AIRSICKNESS BAG
NAPKINS
DRAMAMINE (FROM my stash)
WATER
This is a long day...

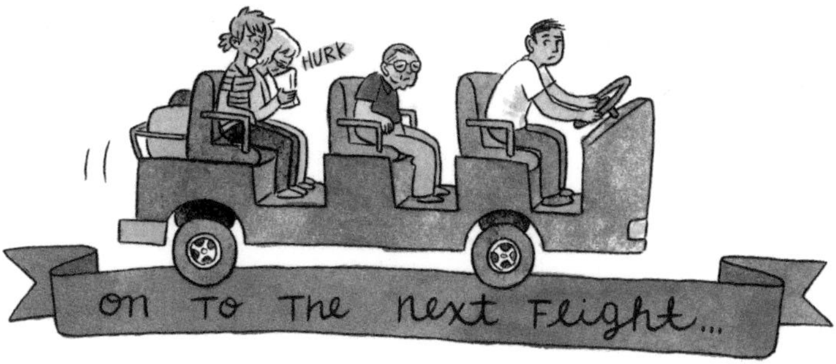
HURK
on to the next Flight...

WHICH IS EXTREMELY

TURBULENT

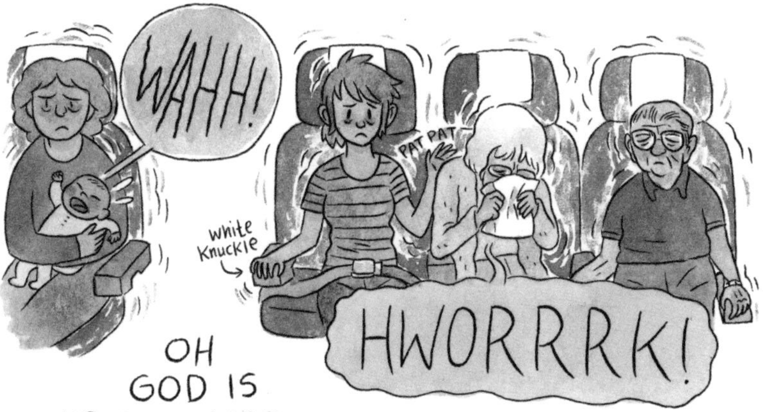
WAHH!
PAT PAT
white Knuckle
HWORRRK!

OH
GOD IS
THIS DAY HAPPENING?

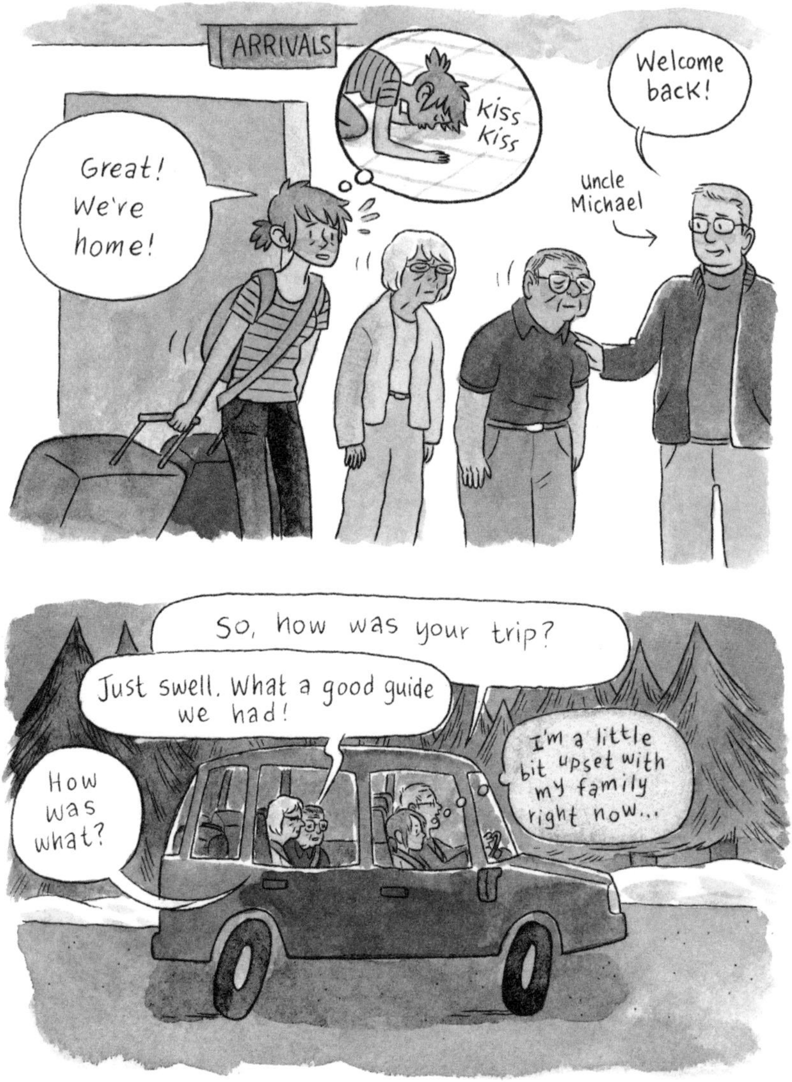
ARRIVALS
Great! We're home!
kiss kiss
Welcome back!
Uncle Michael
So, how was your trip?
Just swell. What a good guide we had!
How was what?
I'm a little bit upset with my family right now...

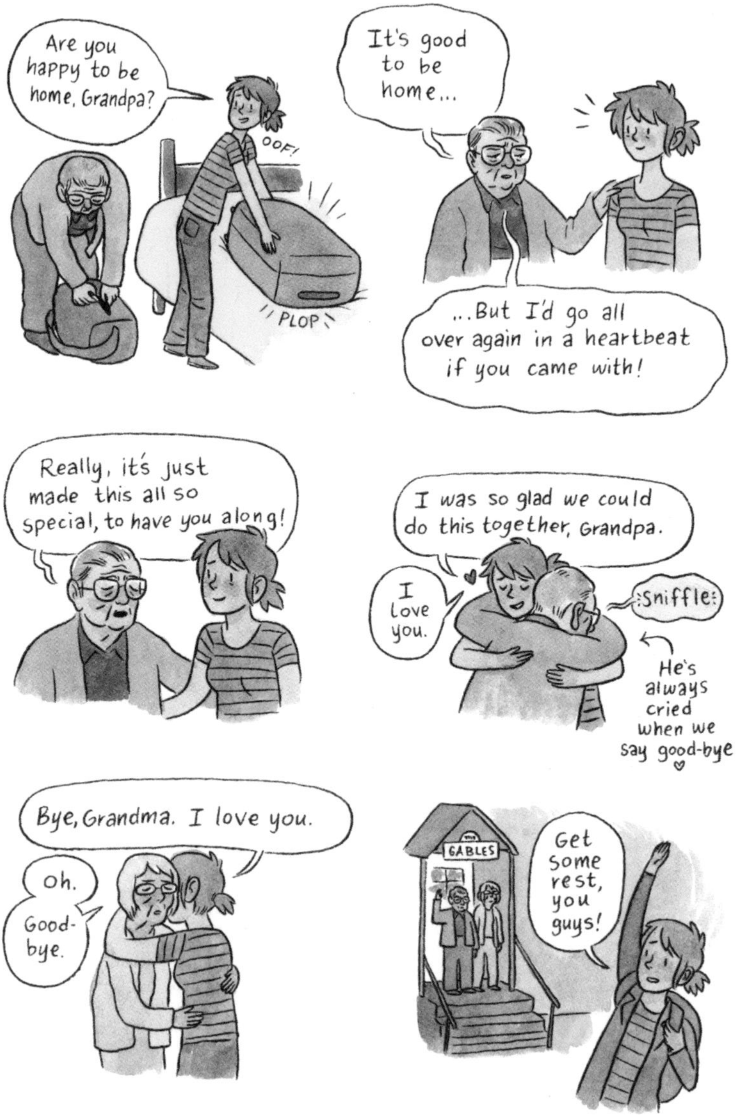
Are you happy to be home, Grandpa?
OOF!
PLOP
It's good to be home...
...But I'd go all over again in a heartbeat if you came with!
Really, it's just made this all so special, to have you along!
I was so glad we could do this together, Grandpa.
I love you.
:Sniffle:
He's always cried when we say good-bye
Bye, Grandma. I love you.
Oh.
Good-bye.
GABLES
Get some rest, you guys!

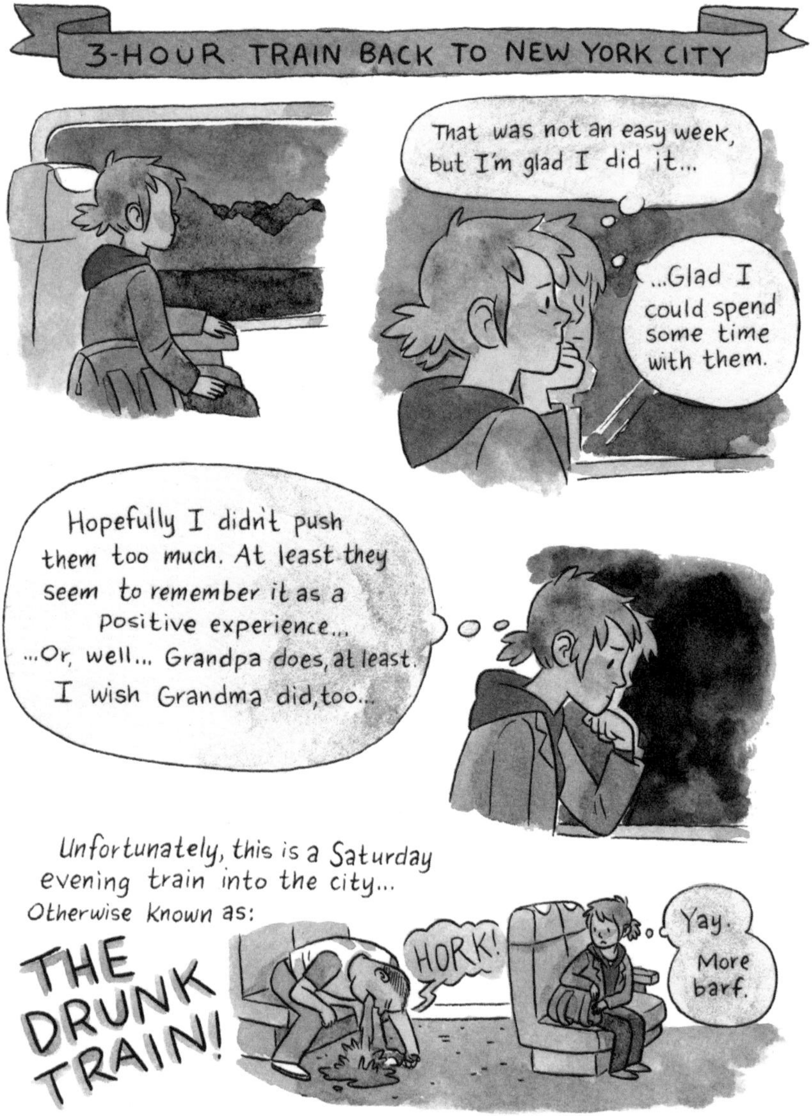
3-HOUR TRAIN BACK TO NEW YORK CITY
That was not an easy week, but I'm glad I did it...
...Glad I could spend some time with them.
Hopefully I didn't push them too much. At least they seem to remember it as a positive experience... ...Or, well... Grandpa does, at least. I wish Grandma did, too...
Unfortunately, this is a Saturday evening train into the city... Otherwise known as:
THE DRUNK TRAIN!
HORK!
Yay. More barf.

At Grand Central Station, I decide to treat myself to a taxi ride home. I'm too exhausted to deal with subways.

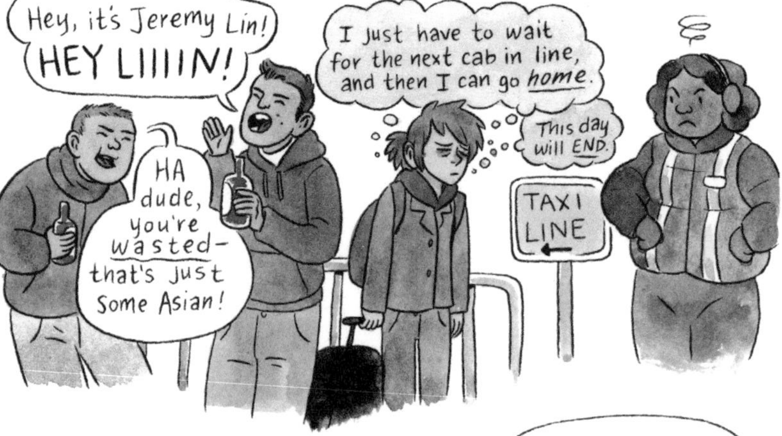
Hey, it's Jeremy Lin! HEY LIIIIN!
HA dude, you're wasted- that's just some Asian!
I just have to wait for the next cab in line, and then I can go home.
This day will END.
TAXI LINE

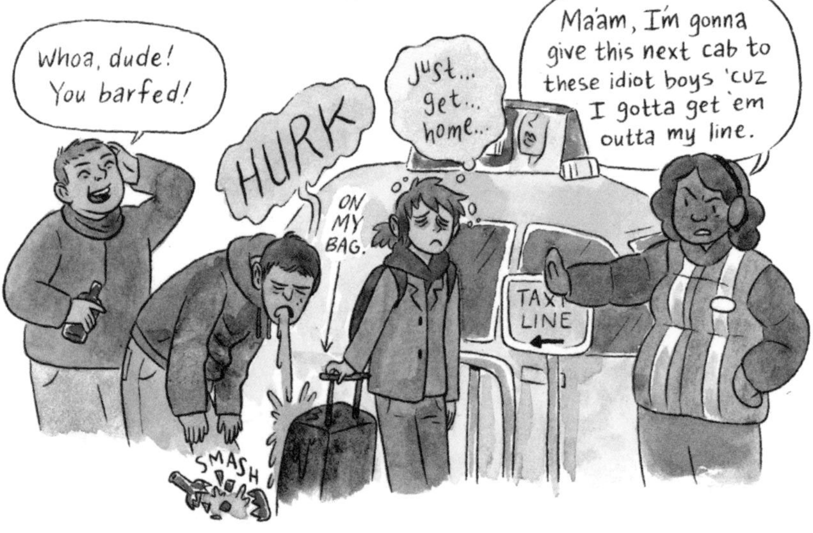
Whoa, dude! You barfed!
HURK
ON MY BAG.
SMASH
Just... get... home...
Ma'am, I'm gonna give this next cab to these idiot boys 'cuz I gotta get 'em outta my line.
TAXI LINE

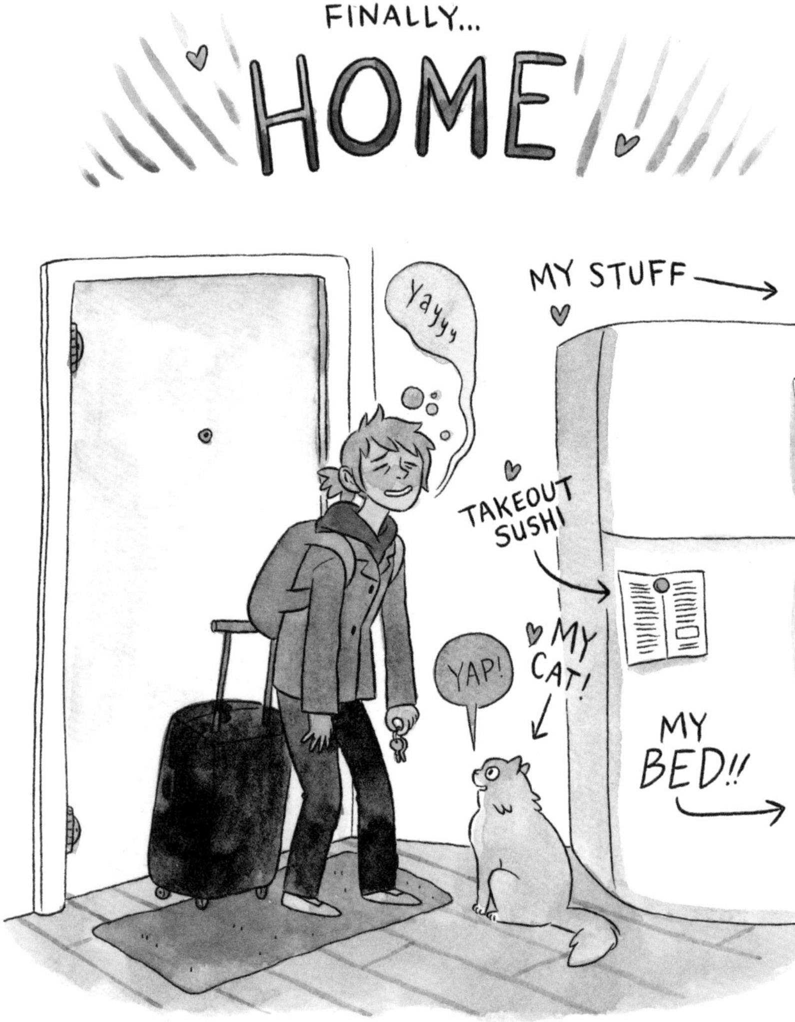
FINALLY...
HOME
Yayyy
MY STUFF
TAKEOUT SUSHI
YAP!
MY CAT!
MY BED!!

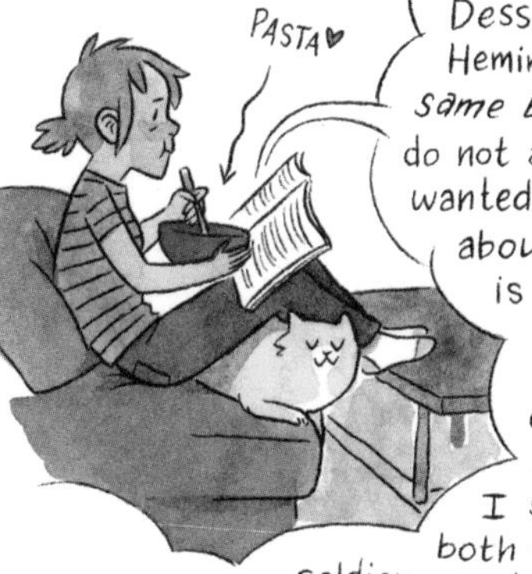
PASTA♥

"I hope I have not misled anyone into thinking that the road from Normandy to Dessau was all glory and fun and games. Hemingway's words, *We all loved the same bitch, and her name was Nostalgia,* do not apply to the war. No one really wanted to die for his country, no one talked about patriotism and bravery. Survival is all we sought.

Since most of the casualties were the result of shelling, death came rather easily. There were not many face-to-face encounters, but I suspect that when they did occur, both the American soldier and German soldier would rather have turned and run from each other. Perhaps many times, they did.

Both the American soldiers and the German soldiers were the same: they hated being where they were, and they hated doing what they were doing. They did not hate each other. *War is the worst invention of mankind.*"

—pg. 50

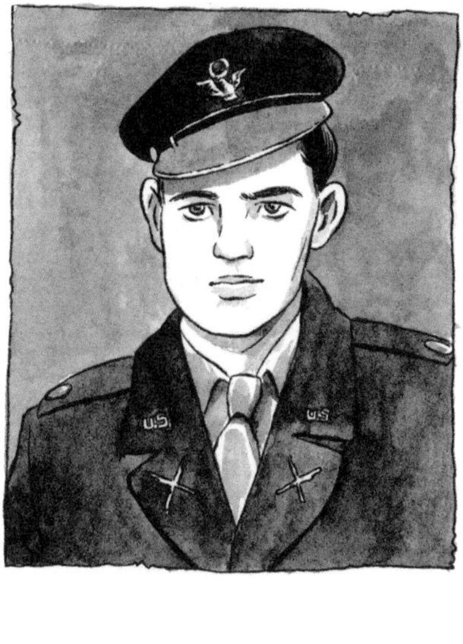
U.S
U.S

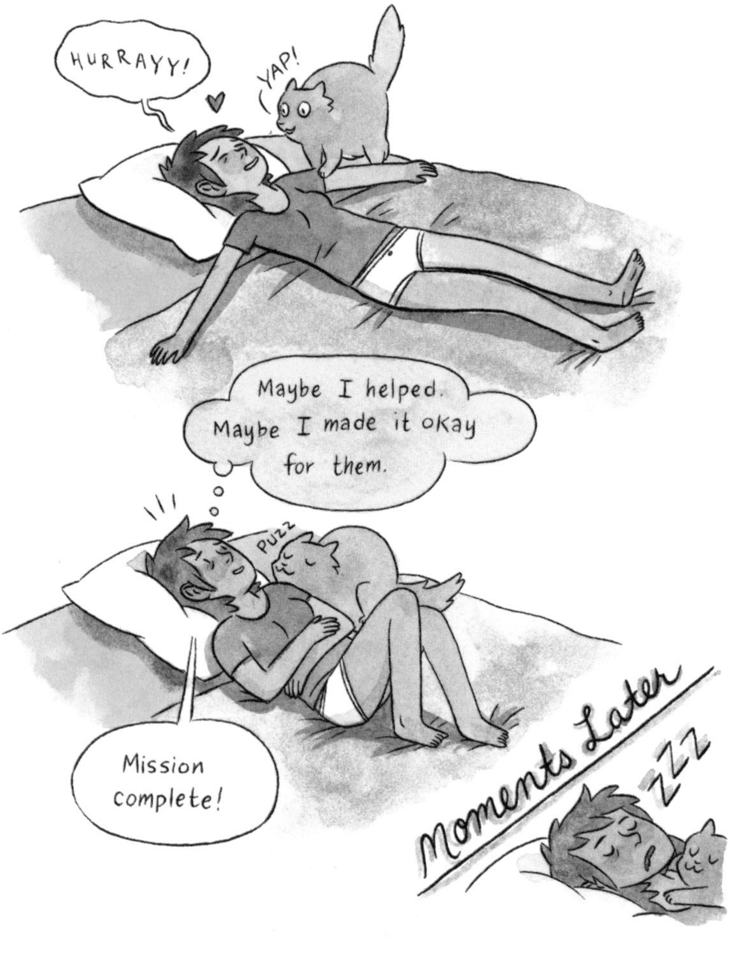
HURRAYY!
YAP!
Maybe I helped. Maybe I made it okay for them.
PUZZ
Mission complete!
Moments Later
ZZZ

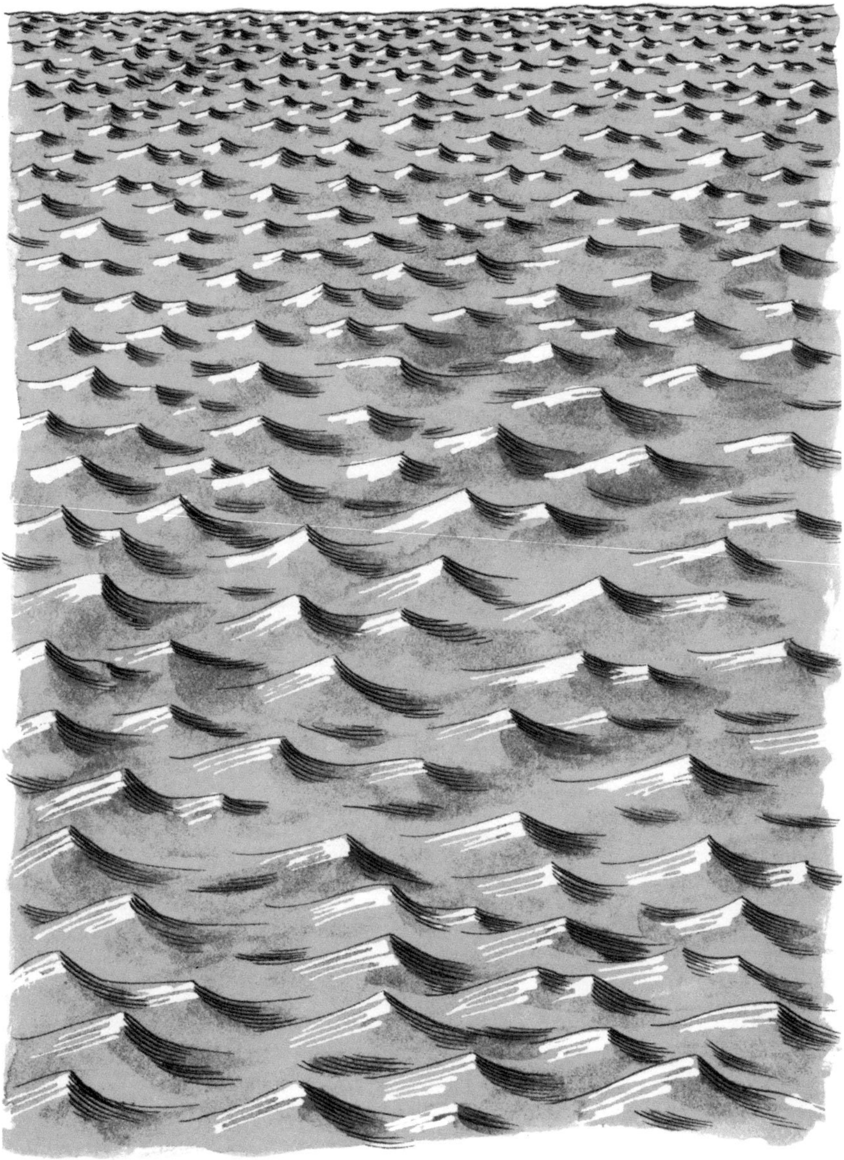

Ever since moving to the city
where my parents lived at my age,
I've been thinking quite a bit
about NOSTALGIA.

PERSONAL and FAMILIAL
HISTORY

Connectivity through space and time and blood.

GOOD OR BAD, IT'S IMPORTANT TO FEEL

CONNECTED

SOMETIMES.

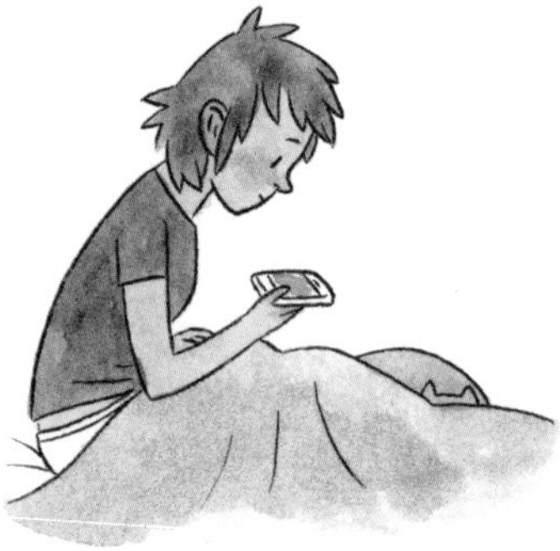

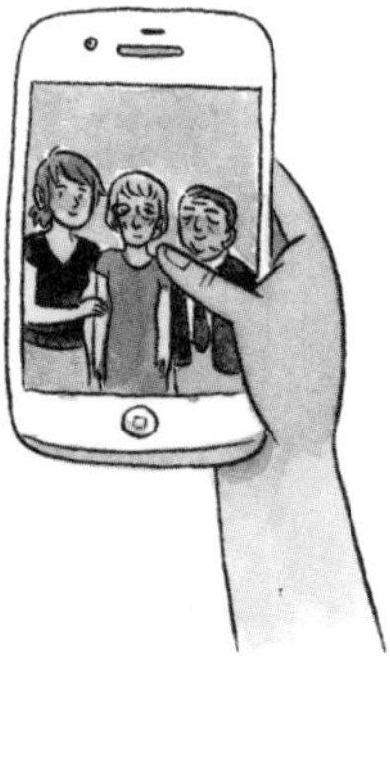

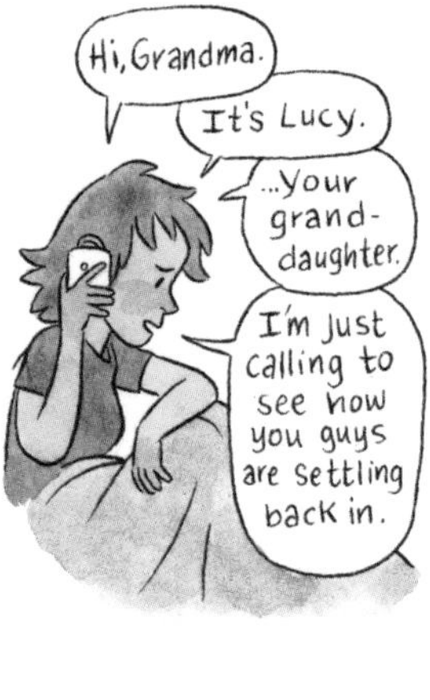
Hi, Grandma.
It's Lucy.
...your grand-daughter.
I'm just calling to see how you guys are settling back in.

Even if that connection can be painful.

Thank you, G & G.

♥, L